Open Thinking in a Closed World

Surviving and Thriving in Alternative Relationships

By Chad Spencer and Melanie Fernandes

Cover by JOLEENE NAYLOR
https://about.me/joleenenaylor

Table of Contents

INTRODUCTION

The quickest way to destroy a relationship is to make it fit into something it is not. Monogamy is a term that humans have used to define their relationships - that we should only be attached to one person for our entire (adult) lives. In fact, we have even tried to justify this label by saying some of the "most noble species" in nature are monogamous - birds of prey, wolves, swans, etc. But now, science has discovered that this term is misapplied to ANY wild species. It simply doesn't occur the way humans understand the term.

Why then, do we continue to make our relationships fit a term that have proven to be, at the very least, misunderstood? Because it's very hard to step outside boxes, pathways and ideas that have been ingrained into our psyches from a young age. Since many people refuse to branch out from what they know, they withhold themselves from relationships that could develop into wonderful experiences.

What if, instead of trying to make our relationships fit outdated and inaccurate models, we took the plunge and opened our minds to the possibility of other relationship styles? If we admitted that for some people monogamy just doesn't work, we could accept that there are other paths to follow. If we acknowledge that we don't just have to choose monogamy to be happy, imagine the possibilities!

ALTERNATIVE RELATIONSHIPS

Since we were born, they surround us by the notion that finding one true love is the key to a happy, fulfilled life. We grow up with this imbedded in our brains, so most people think that is how things truly should be. This thought prevails despite humans performing horribly at long-term monogamy. Did you know that humans are one of the very few species on this planet that practice monogamy? In looking back through the history of human existence, we can see that monogamy has represented quite a small percentage of human history because of the simple biological fact that humans are not meant to be monogamous. This counters what many people think in society today because monogamy is all that many people have grown up knowing. When that is all that most of us see in our families, in society, in TV and the movies, etc., it is hard for people to grasp concepts that go against all that we are conditioned to believe.

Contrary to these atmospheres, not only has monogamy not been widespread for most of history, but it is only one of various options in society today. Monogamy is in fact, a made-up construct, related to gender roles and social order. It does not represent a stronger commitment to a person, rather a strong commitment to a principle–the principle of monogamy. Is a polyamorous couple together for 20 years any less committed to each other just because they occasionally see other people? If you think that they are less committed to each other, why do you think that? Because they are not fully exclusive to each other? They have established a connection with each other over the years, but have chosen not to limit themselves to only seeing one person. 20 years is a long time to have anyone in your life, and that takes a lot of commitment, regardless of any other activities going on in both lives.

Perhaps the best place to discuss the contents of this book is to glance at a few terms that are confusing and/or mistaken for polyamory.

Ethical non-monogamy (also known as open relationship) is perhaps the broadest term that applies to alternative relationship paths. It means that a set of primary partners have agreed to a set of rules/guidelines that allows for both parties involved in a relationship to know that the other is choosing to see other people. The key word is "ethical". Everything occurs with the consent and knowledge of BOTH parties. Open relationships/ethical non-monogamy allows couples to continue to acknowledge that they have the urge/need to see other people without the need to cheat and lie. It requires that both partners be open minded and communicate often and fairly with their partner(s) to ensure that all parties remain happy.

Ethical non-monogamy can encompass a lot of different lifestyles. Since one focus of this book is polyamory, lets define it - Poly = many, Amory = love. Polyamory = "Many loves". Such a simple definition for a term that is so often misunderstood.

Polyamory is about forming multiple loving relationships. It is *not* about having as many sexual partners as possible. That is a more casual dating thing, which polyamory can inappropriately get lumped into by some. Polyamory is more about finding and making strong connections with other people. Polyamorous people do not equate sex with love, and they will not "end" a relationship because chemistry isn't instantaneous, or sex isn't a fantastic experience.

Every relationship has different qualities, and while many follow a similar trajectory, each relationship involves certain miscellaneous specifics. For most people, the usual pattern is to date people they are interested in, continue to see and develop certain good connections with one or some, and ultimately attempt a long-term, sometimes lifetime partnership with a particular chosen one. This works for some couples, has become a standard goal for many, and is a standard that many people think of as the best goal to strive for. Just like every person is different in certain ways though, most couples, and how they connect with each other differ from other couples too. Should every couple that has a great connection, seclude themselves from seeing anyone else, and only date each other? This is often the setup of many serious romantic relationships. Why do modern humans, as a supposedly intelligent, evolved species make guidelines that treat interest in any other human as a failure to the human you develop a strong connection with? Once we find a connection with another person, and it interests both in seeing each other more, modern society has led us to believe that we should close ourselves off from anyone else romantically.

It is exciting when you first establish a great connection with someone. Both of you can't wait to see each other, and everything seems great. You have fun sharing various activities together, then being intimate together, learning more and more about each other. These are exciting times. You are both attracted to each other, are having a lot of fun together, and everything seems great. This new relationship energy (NRE) happens in the beginning of great connections. Not every two people that date have perfect connections, but for the many that do, these can be some of the most exciting times. You share these incredible experiences together, and everything seems great. Thoughts pop in your head to share more and more of these exciting times with that person. Why wouldn't you think that? You might see a lot of this person in the beginning, and that could mean that you are only dating this person for a period, and no one else. We only have so much free time, so you might maximize this free time of yours by spending it the best way– with this great new connection. That could work out well, but many situations also have other details involved.

Dan and Carrie started seeing each other and instantly connected. They were attracted to each other, shared the same values, and had a great time together. They experienced new relationship energy and saw each other twice a week for a few weeks, getting closer and closer. Both of them got caught up in this new relationship energy, and neither had yet discussed any other circumstances going on in their lives. They were not hiding anything, but just had not found it relevant yet to bring up anyone else. They were getting a feel where things were with each other and enjoying every minute.

Before meeting Dan, Carrie had a casual relationship with her friend Tom over the past year. They had become good friends, saw each other occasionally, and also had great sex. They didn't follow society's standard narrative of becoming an exclusive "couple" for multiple reasons, mostly because they wanted to see other people while still keeping their friendship strong. Some would call this relationship "friends with benefits", but Tom and Carrie had been friends for a while now, and never called it anything. Tom was dating a few girls, but hadn't quite met a connection as great as the one Carrie and Dan were having, nor was he trying for that.

When Carrie meets Dan, sparks fly, and they have an incredible start. She temporarily disbands other social elements out of her life while she starts her great association with Dan. Carrie and Dan are developing such a great connection that many in their situation would become an exclusive couple and start calling each other boyfriend and girlfriend. To enter an exclusive relationship with Dan, this would mean Carrie would have to stop seeing Tom (and any other male she was interested in). She is really into Dan, but has known Tom for a year, had some great times with him, and still was having great sex with him before she met Dan. She should give up seeing Tom because things are so great with Dan? Some would ask why she needs to see Tom now that she has Dan. Just because things with Dan are great does not mean that she won't miss seeing Tom though. Just like every person is different, every relationship is different, and every great connection is different. Even though Carrie is crazy about Dan now, that has not lessened her feelings for Tom or her experiences with him.

Love is not limited, and even if she is falling in love with Dan, whatever feelings that she has for Tom can co-exist. She may experience different loves, but her feelings for both men are very important to Carrie, so she feels that they should treat neither feeling less than the other. If things get more serious between Dan and Carrie, they should discuss other things in their lives to ensure that they are on the same page with how they handle those elements.

Dan did not know about Tom being in Carrie's life the past year. How could he? He did not know Carrie before they met. As she saw things getting more serious, Carrie came forward and told Dan about Tom to see how he felt. She was interested in both how he would react to hearing about it, and how he would react to the possibility of her seeing Tom still. She had no idea how Dan would react since they had not known each other until recently, but his reaction happily surprised her.

Upon hearing about Tom, Dan acknowledged that Carrie and Tom's relationship existed before he even knew Carrie, and he also accepted how quickly his connection with Carrie has developed. Instead of getting jealous and asking her not to see Tom anymore, Dan told Carrie that whatever happened, he wanted her happy first. Second, he did not want her to have to sacrifice anything for him. If he and Carrie kept seeing each other, whatever was meant to happen between them, would happen. She was surprised at how unselfish his reaction was based on what she was used to seeing in society, but having quickly gotten to know Dan, she was ultimately not surprised by Dan putting Carrie and their relationship before anything else. Dan was not just being unselfish though. He had learned a lot from his relationship experience earlier in life, deciding on a life change.

Dan followed the standard relationship escalator pattern his whole life because that is all he knew. Dan had dated a lot growing up, some of the relationships lasting months, some of them a few years. Carrie knew Dan had married and divorced before, but did not quite know just how his relationships over the years had shaped him. After his divorce, Dan dated again, and started into the same pattern of connecting well with some, then ultimately breaking up and seeing others. This was all Dan knew, and he was happy most of the time, so he kept going through his usual dating patterns.

After doing this for a while, he realized that at some point in time after some of his relationships ended, he wanted to see some of his exes again (even if he was the one that had ended it before). He got back together with some of them, but ultimately ended them again. This happened to him enough times that he recognized the pattern and wanted to stop the continuous relationship cycles. He had heard a little about alternative relationships, and how people were choosing other relationship styles (including seeing multiple people) while still in what seemed on the surface "standard" relationships. This alternative relationship concept intrigued him so he started learning more about them and discovered open relationships and polyamory. He had started by reading the alternative relationship "bible"–'The Ethical Slut', then on to 'Redefining Our Relationships', 'Opening Up', and 'Stepping off the Relationship Escalator'. He quickly discovered that he had not ended his relationships with the girls he was dating because there was anything wrong with them, but simply because he wanted to see other people at times.

Why did he have to end a great relationship with a girl he was dating just because he was interested in occasionally seeing other girls? Even if he went on a date with another girl, that would subtract nothing from the connection he had with his existing girlfriend. Mainstream society did not groom him that way though, so he never thought of that as an option. Upon discovering this possibility, he learned the true benefits of open relationships, instead of just always following the standard monogamous setup. Dan continued to research and absorb more about this open relationship lifestyle, and he experienced the benefits of seeing multiple people, but also learning how it involved more work than a standard monogamous relationship.

Seeing multiple people enabled Dan to satisfy different aspects of his life. Open relationships follow different formats. In Dan's case, he had his primary relationship first. He was best friends, lovers, and shared responsibilities with this girl, but also had different connections elsewhere with different girls. These other girls have different personalities, different appearances, and offered different experiences to Dan's life overall. He could enjoy different lives with a few different people, instead of just one life with one person.

At first, some people that only knew standard monogamy setups questioned this open relationship lifestyle, and even joked that Dan was "having his cake and eating it too". This ignored the fact that having more friendships in his life also involved some effort and time considerations too. Seeing how happy both he and his primary partner were, however, these people had to acknowledge that they were doing something right. Dan sometimes responded to people that questioned him having more "friends" in his life. Different friends bring different connections and experiences in his life. "These are different though" some would say. "How is it different?" he asked. "Because of sex?" Any girl Dan saw besides his primary, he was friends with first. Whether he became intimate with any of them did not change any of Dan's relationships, including his primary relationship. Things were still great between him and his primary partner, regardless if he saw anyone else. Dan spent the most time with his primary partner, never deceived her, and always gave her the utmost respect. If either of them was unhappy with anything in their relationship, they would talk about it, and work out an amicable solution. Again, different open relationships have different styles. Some have no primary partners, some have one primary partner, and some have multiple primary partners. As in any relationship style in life though, with communication, trust, and mutual consent between the members, any relationship can flourish.

Back to Carrie now. She knew a little of Dan's past life, but not the details, like how Dan had learned that it is not rational to expect one person to supply all the emotional, physical, and psychological components in a relationship, no matter how incredible that person is. Even the most intelligent, the most beautiful, or the best anything quality in a person cannot escape the simple fact that it is still the SAME one person. Dan had learned this, and that is why he accepted Carrie seeing Tom still. He knew that no matter how great of a connection he and Carrie had developed, that he could not be EVERYTHING to Carrie, so he wanted her to see others too. He wanted to keep these exciting feelings alive with Carrie, and he had learned what many others do not acknowledge - that this NRE excitement ALWAYS fades over time in a monogamous relationship.

While the excitement might fade a little in an open, non-monogamous relationship as well, that will not happen as fast because it keeps the spark alive and "fresh" by not seeing each other too often, or exclusively. Not seeing each other too much allows people to miss each other. Dan learned the importance of missing the girls he was seeing, and he wanted to keep that feeling going with Carrie. In the past, he had not missed the girls that he dated exclusively. That is not taking anything away from those girls because they were wonderful, but since they were exclusive, they saw each other regularly. Not only did he see his partner regularly, but without seeing any other girl. This was great in the beginning with the NRE, but relationships become stable and normalize. Missing someone isn't possible when you see the same person all the time. Dan knew this, so even though he was crazy about Carrie, he did not want to see her all the time and let their relationship fall into any kind of lull.

Both sides of a relationship often feel excitement in the beginning, and most everything can seem incredible, even perfect. This is the fun, new relationship energy that many people experience, and it is a great thing. People fall into the trap of thinking this new relationship energy will last forever, or even a long time, but it does not. Even the best connections don't stay exciting forever. That isn't trying to downplay the great connections, because great connections aren't common either. How people handle these great connections, or any connection is the topic to discuss.

What do you do if you go on a date with someone and there is no connection? You likely don't see that person again. If the opposite is happening, and you both feel a perfect connection, does that mean that couples should do the opposite, and see each other all the time? When great connections are established, many people have followed what became the standard relationship structure–they date, become exclusive if the connection develops, move in together, marriage, children.

Most times, it is beneficial to keep positive relationships in your life, so it makes sense to keep seeing the people that you have great connections with. What makes little sense, is the exclusivity part of this common relationship structure. There is a combination of reasons for exclusive relationships from jealousy to the simple reason that it is how many people are raised, so it is all they know. A lot of us don't even think of any other options. We meet, date, become exclusive, and either take the next step and get married, or eventually break up.

Sometimes we see more than one person, and we call that "dating". We treat that as casual, whereas if the same two people keep seeing each other, it would be taken more seriously. If this progressed, they would be a "couple", and most likely not date anyone else. These exclusive couples are taken more seriously than people that are casually dating, and in many ways, justifiably so. Having a strong bond with someone can be an incredible thing, but does that mean that you should limit yourself, and not see anyone else? That incredible spark you have with your partner in the beginning is a combination of not just the great connection between you and your partner, but also the novelty of it. Once you commit for an extended time to this one partner, you only have the great connection part of that spark, with the novelty vanishing. People have suggested various ways to keep that spark alive, from role play, to romantic evenings, to doing different activities together. Those might add a little something, but often not for long.

These various "spark" tactics still cannot ignore the fact that whatever you do, it is still with the same person. You are looking at the same face, hearing the same voice, kissing the same lips, being intimate with the same body. Notwithstanding how incredible that person is, the simple fact remains–it is the same person. No matter how much you mix up activities together, everything moderates over time. You have more than one platonic friend, right? Culture has raised us to have many friends, and having many friends introduces different elements into our lives, good, bad, and in between. Being exposed to different elements helps us grow in life, learn, evolve, and ultimately become happier. Different friends help bring these different elements into our lives, so we shouldn't close ourselves off to this exposure, right? But we should limit ourselves to just one person in our romantic relationships? Why do we have as many platonic friends as possible, but most people limit themselves to one person in romantic relationships? One word - sex.

People limit themselves in so many ways because of that one word. So, we hang out with our platonic friends, and do activities with any of these friends with no problems, but the moment things get serious with someone you are dating, you cannot be intimate with anyone else? Society says a person can be intimate with other people if all the relationships are considered "casual". The minute one of them turns more than just casual, that is when you must cut off friendly times with anyone else you were being intimate with. Society even takes it a step further. You don't just have to cut off intimate relationships with other people once you get into a romantic relationship with someone, you cut off ALL types of contact with anyone that you were intimate with before. When you are in a relationship, you can't even be casual friends with someone that you had sex with before the relationship. Why? Because if anyone saw or heard that you were even near someone that you were intimate with before, they immediately think "they must be fucking".

Another word comes into play with monogamous relationships–possession. Think about it. When people are together, it can feel appropriate for one partner to say to the other "you're mine". People in love embrace that thought in a positive manner, but that is a form of possession.

John and Emily have been in a relationship for two years, so most of their friends think of them as "John's girl", or "Emi's dude". This is common knowledge to friends and family and seems normal to everyone.

What does that mean though? It means two people involve themselves significantly in each other's lives as opposed to casually dating. Being significantly involved in someone's life means each partner has input, sometimes very large input into everything in the other person's life. That can be something as minor as cleaning the house, what to have for dinner, or what movie to see. It can also be something major like who the other person hangs out with, what they do, or where and when they go places. Often in serious relationships, most anything you do in your life, you share. The biggest restriction out of that who, what, when, and where is the *who*.

Despite a small percentage increase in the other direction with the young crowd, most romantic relationships are still monogamous. In these monogamous relationships, who you can see is the biggest restriction. People in a relationship can see most platonic friends with no questions, but cannot see anyone, friends or not, that he or she has been previously intimate with. Standard platonic friendships don't have restrictions on who a person can and cannot see, but any possibility of intimacy raises barriers.

There may be some platonic friends who don't care for other friends, but they just wouldn't associate with them, not restrict you from doing so. Romantic relationships have these restrictions though, and not just one or two people–ANYONE that you have or would be intimate with. As soon as a heterosexual male becomes involved in a monogamous relationship, most every one of the 3 billion other females on the planet mind as well not exist, because outside of family, this guy can do no more than say hi to any girl before questions arise. If he even gets friendly with another female, he is a jerk because he is breaking the monogamous couple's unspoken agreement of his partner being the only girl for him now. He is "hers".

Think about if some random guy finds your girlfriend attractive. If he did not know the girl was involved, he might flirt and make some moves on the girl. Even if he knew she was involved, he might make a move anyway, but that's a different story. If the girl is interested, but still refuses, she would say something like "sorry, I can't, I'm seeing someone", or "sorry, I'm taken", or "No, I'm John's girl". What if this girl was interested in this guy though? Or what if SHE makes a move? Two people interested in getting to know each other more, but the monogamous rule of thumb is that they need to refrain from that because one of them is in a relationship.

This monogamy agreement is supposed to be in place for as long as the couple is together. What if they are together for 10 years? For 10 years, both only experience intimacy with each other under monogamy guidelines. Everyone else in the world is forbidden to them. What if Emily gets overcome with desire for someone else, and she then becomes intimate with another guy? What does this change in her 10-year relationship with Johnny? Because she was intimate one time with someone else, that should end a 10-year loving relationship? Why? Even if she took part in a physical act with someone else, her feelings have not changed for John at home. She was excited about experiencing the novelty of this intimate time with someone else that she had been attracted to, and she acted on it. She still wakes up the next day and loves John the same.

Because Emily satisfied a craving for someone different after only being with the same guy for 10 years, many people would shame her for this, even though nothing overall changed because of this one occurrence. So, because she had sex with Paul, that means she feels nothing for Johnny anymore, and they should split? Some would say that she broke their agreement and now cannot be trusted. If she did this once, chances are she would do it again. While it is true that she broke an agreement if they did not talk about this ahead of time, the important issue of trust is her not hiding this from John. If they had indeed talked about it ahead of time though, and shared what they both wanted, they can both fully enjoy their lives together, knowing the other is happy without restrictions.

Some people would immediately end a relationship if their partner was intimate with anyone else. If your partner did this behind your back, that is deceitful, but what if you knew about this same act ahead of time? You knew your partner was seeing someone else at times, so there was a potential for intimacy, but things remain the same between you two. Occasional times with other people, whether or not it includes physical acts, does not affect a primary relationship if both people mutually agree to it. Your partner has most likely had sex with people before you two knew each other, but now after you two have been intimate, he or she cannot be intimate with anyone else? What would that change? Many people still shake their head, "nope, don't want my partner sleeping around." This is understandable if it affected your relationship, but the occasional experience with someone else rarely takes anything away from a primary relationship. If the relationship was strong before, it remains just as good. If the relationship had problems before, the same problems will exist. People simply overthink certain outside occurrences. If a couple is truly open and wants each other fully happy, then they could have peace of mind in knowing that the person he or she loves is happy, both from his or her life within the relationship, and with life outside of the relationship.

After talking ahead of time about her desires, John knew that Emily is occasionally interested in seeing people besides her platonic friends. Regardless of what this is for, just because it is with someone of the opposite sex, Emily wants to have the option of seeing these people without affecting her strong relationship with John. She might have lunch with a male co-worker, go on a date with a male friend, have passionate sex, just a kiss, or basically anything she wants. Emily had the right to do what she wanted when she was single. She wants the same rights to do what she wants now. In monogamous relationships, as soon as you are even a little involved with someone, those rights to do whatever you want are gone. Now you must check in and consider how the other person feels about your choices.

Emily followed this arrangement in the beginning, because that was the standard, and what she knew. After a while though, Emily missed the simple freedom of doing what she wanted and seeing who she wanted to see. She did not just do anything with no consideration for the situation though, as she had a talk with John about how she felt. She loved him and knew they were great together, but she felt that even though she wanted to continue to see him, and they were having no problems together, she wanted neither of them to ever limit themselves and not live life to the fullest. John and Emily were very compatible together. They enjoyed each other's company, were very attracted to each other, and had great sex. They hardly ever fought either. There were no problems. Emily just knew that over the years, things level out, and the excitement fades.

Most everyone that she knew accepted that and didn't do much about it because that had become normal couple life. The few people that she knew that experienced exciting other times, did so by cheating on their partner, and she did not want to be deceitful like that. She remembered the time when she and John met, and the exciting times they had together. She also remembered the exciting times she had with other guys that she dated, just like John had with the girls he dated. Emily wasn't looking to end the great relationship with John but wanted some of that excitement from before too. Some of her conventional friends suggested doing different things with John, mixing things up. She tried to explain to her friends that they HAD mixed things up over the years and had fun together. That wasn't the point. It was still with the same person over the years, so that is a different excitement. She pointed out that nothing was changing between her and John. They were adding to their lives. Besides, sometimes seeing other people makes a person miss the partner he or she has that much more. Some of her friends got this, some didn't. The ones that didn't get it just could not wrap their heads around something different, only because they had never seen it before.

After Emily shared her thoughts with John, she reinforced how she wanted things to stay the same between them. She just wanted them both to be on the same page that it was ok to see other people and not have to hide it. John listened to this and acknowledged that while there is nothing wrong with their relationship, occasional encounters out of the house could be exciting. John knew the fact that even though their relationship is great, he is still just one person. The fact remains that he cannot fully satisfy every desire of another person, no matter how awesome he is. No one can.

Any of us might have an incredible connection with someone in multiple ways, but no one has a perfect connection with someone in every way. So how do we resolve that? People date to test their connections with people, and the people they think they are well matched with, they see again. If these strong connections continue to be true, then they become a couple. Just because these two people had multiple connections and became partners though, does that mean they are perfect together? Nope. Because they have multiple connections, does that mean a light switch goes off in their bodies, and they have no desires for anyone else? Nope. Monogamous couples try to flip that switch though, and as soon as they become a couple, close themselves off from intimacy with anyone else in the world. Why? Is intimacy with someone else a threat between two partners? What about their abundant connections together? If one is intimate with someone else, do these many connections vanish?

Just because Emily and John were an exceptional match together, Emily now must choose whether she wants a relationship with John, or still occasionally see other people? She does not feel like she must choose one or the other. Things can stay phenomenal with John, while she occasionally sees other people still. Some people might say that she should just keep things casual with John then so they can both see other people. Why do they have to keep things casual for that option though? They developed strong connections and want to spend more time together, but they must stay casual for the option to see other people? Time can be a factor and if Emily and John are spending more time together, they have less time for other people, but that doesn't mean they have to eliminate that option from their life. If Emily and John agree on their options together, they should still have the option to see who they want.

Let's look at the other side of things and pretend that Emily restricted herself, like monogamy says she should. Even though she was tempted at times by other men during her relationship with John, if she remained loyal and did not see anyone else, isn't there a possibility that she grows resentful because she did not act on something she wanted? This resentment might grow and cause her to become bitter towards John, or to the relationship in general. This change in attitude could manifest itself into other things, like occasional arguing, not wanting intimacy with John, or slowly becoming more and more unhappy. That might not happen with everyone, but it is a possibility. How do you react if you don't get something you want? What if your partner prevented you from getting something you wanted? You would completely accept that and not be the least bit bitter? What if your partner did the opposite and gave you what you wanted?

Johnny told her, yeah, have fun, honey, but just stay clean and get home safe. Many people would say "how can he let his girl see, and maybe be intimate with someone else?" or "nope, that would bother me thinking about her with someone else." Those are normal responses but take a step back and think about that for a second. Why does that bother you if your partner sees other people, or was intimate with someone else? Are you worried that it would change things between you both? You think John should worry about Emily leaving him for another guy? You think she would give up 10 years with John, whom she loved, just because she occasionally saw others, or even sometimes had a night of great sex with someone else? What really is the concern here? Do you get worried about others being better than you? That is a confidence thing, and something you need to address with yourself, not worry about from other people.

Many people think relationships change after someone sleeps with someone else but ask yourself how it changed. Instead of being a couple over the past 10 years, say Johnny and Emily were not a couple, and simply knew each other. They went out, doing things here and there, and occasionally had sex. If either of them slept with anyone else, it wouldn't be a big deal at all (if they stayed clean). If they both enjoyed their meetups, they might increase the frequency. Often when two people see each other more, a switch turns on in their heads, and they decide "let's be a couple". As soon as they turn on that switch, they also turn off the possibility of sleeping with anyone else in their lives. That might not matter to them when things are exciting, and they experience that new relationship energy in the beginning. What about after dating exclusively for a while though? Emily missed the novelty of those new relationship exciting times, and she also missed the great sex she was having with another guy before she became exclusive with Johnny. Because she and John were exclusive for the past 10 years though, she could no longer sleep with this other guy. Emily was restricting herself the exciting times with others because of the monogamy principle.

If she was really into this other guy that she had sex with before John, then she should date him you think? Maybe this other guy and Emily had great times together, but still wanted to have great times with other people as well. They kept seeing each other but saw other people as well. They both were thrilled with this arrangement. Then Emily met John, and John seemed more traditional at first, so she gave just John a try, taking a break from the other guy. Time goes on, life happens, but just because she is really compatible with John, she has to permanently give up the great sex she had with the other guy? Or anyone else for that matter? Could she not still have a great relationship with Johnny while occasionally satisfying a certain desire with the other guy? If she did that, she would still have the great life with Johnny, while not denying herself the occasional great times with the other guy (or others).

Joe and Lisa

Joe and Lisa have been dating for 5 years, very comfortable with where things were in the relationship, and both did not want children. Even though things were great in the relationship in all aspects, the discussion of seeing other people came up. Joe discussed seeing other people occasionally, while he and Lisa remained together as a primary couple.

Take the role of Lisa and choose her response based on what would be most like your response:

Choice 1: Absolutely refuse to either of them seeing other people. If Joe wants to see other people, he can be single again.

Result of Choice 1: It upset Lisa with Joe mentioning seeing other people and she interpreted it as him wanting other girls. She did not see any benefits of opening the relationship to other people and kept focusing on how she did not want Joe seeing other girls. Despite Joe assuring her that things would not change between them, Lisa kept insisting that it be just her, and no one else. Joe complied to this at first, but considering that he still was interested in seeing other people, he wasn't happy. He did not take any immediate action and do anything rash though. He did more research on opening the relationship, and the benefits that it could provide. Six months later when he casually brought up some of the things that he learned about open relationships, Lisa still wouldn't budge and became upset that he was still thinking about this. Joe did not want to upset Lisa anymore, nor be unhappy anymore, so he ended things with Lisa and began seeing other girls. He told Lisa that there was nothing wrong in their relationship, except for the fact that they limited it to one person. Joe had discovered that while this monogamy scenario can work for some people, it was not something that he was completely into. Different things work for different people. Since Lisa did not want to give Joe's request a chance at all, he felt that it forced him to end things, so both could pursue total happiness with what they wanted.

Choice 2: Consider Joe's suggestion, but since you aren't really into it, he can try it occasionally, but with restraint and respect to the relationship first.

Result of Choice 2: Lisa listened to Joe's suggestion of opening their relationship to other people, and while the idea intrigued her a little, there was no one else that she was currently interested in. Lisa was currently busy with work and getting her health in order, so she was not interested in seeing other people at this time. She did not want to hold Joe back from occasionally seeing others though, so she suggested he try it at times, if it did not interfere with many things in their life. Joe was happy that Lisa was being open-minded about the idea because he did truly care about their relationship, but simply wanted to exercise the normal human urge to see others at times. He did not want to be restricted from members of the opposite sex just because he was in a great relationship.

Joe started seeing other people, occasional new dates here and there, and rekindling with some of the people he saw before he met Lisa. Joe was happy with having the occasional night out, and he did this while remaining respectful to Lisa. He brought no one to their house, he stayed clean, and anytime he drank, he made sure that he got home safely. Some of Lisa's friends did not understand how she seemed so fine with Joe seeing other people. She told them that thinking about it wasn't always 100% easy, but her main concern was just that he got home safe when he went out. The fact that he was occasionally seeing other girls changed nothing between them, and she knew that they both still loved each other very much. This great love between Lisa and Joe did not change regardless if Joe went out alone, went out with male friends, or went out with female friends. As proof of this, Joe and Lisa tried this setup for two years, and since everything in their relationship continued to be just as strong as before, they continued this alternative relationship style for another 10 years and counting.

Throughout those years, no one outside the relationship (besides the close friends that they told) knew about their alternative relationship style, and only perceived them as a regular, happy couple. Just like in a standard relationship setup, there were some occasional challenging times, but as they had always done, they talked through everything, and made sure that they respected the other person's viewpoints. Because of this strong communication and full trust in each other, Joe and Lisa continued to have an elated life together, regardless of their relationship style. Joe met a mix of people, some that were open to seeing Joe despite his situation at home, some who wanted nothing to do with him because of his situation at home, some who became friends, some lovers, some text buddies, and some platonic friends. Joe was respectful to all involved, and found that instead of needing to know where things were going with anyone he met, he was just happy to have new experiences with new people, and enjoyed his life. One thing he learned from meeting new people is that it was not about the destination with that person, but about the journey. Every person he met did not have to involve a plan or a target. If they wanted to see each other again, they did. If not, then it was still most likely a positive experience.

Choice 3: Accept Joe's suggestion to mix up the relationship, and agree that both will try it, while still respecting their relationship as the primary.

Result of Choice 3: Lisa agreed to the thought of opening their relationship because she was curious how it would work. She knew that they were a strong couple, so their great communication and trust in each other would continue, despite the setup change.

They both agreed that they each would have one night per week on average of doing whatever they wanted. This could include anything from going out for drinks and a meal by yourself, going out with friends, or going out on dates. They agreed that whatever each of them wanted to do on their night out was fine if they stayed STD clean and got home safe. Both started seeing other people, and both seemed happy with this arrangement at first. Each of them knew when the other was going out, often on a date, but they did not want to know the details. All Lisa and Joe cared about was being respectful to all involved and honoring the agreement of staying clean and safe. They loved each other and knew that occasional experiences with other people would not change that love. Lisa and Joe both honored this agreement, and their new relationship style started off well. Both were seeing other people occasionally, having new experiences, and continuing as the same close knit, happy couple at home.

This continued for a year, and then Lisa became close to one guy she was seeing. This guy knew her situation at home, was fine with it, but had also fallen in love with Lisa. Lisa still honors her agreement with Joe, but finds that she has fallen in love with Brett as well. Meanwhile, Joe is taking a break from seeing other people for a bit. He is busy with work, and trying to improve his health by going to the gym more, while saving money at the same time. Since he takes a break from going out on his own for a bit, Lisa occasionally goes out an extra night during the week. This allows her to do more of whatever she wants on her own, including seeing Brett more. Lisa and Brett have some nights out with just drinks and laughs, some nights with hot intimacy back at his place, and some nights out to dinner. They seem like a happy duo when they are together, because they are happy together. They also do not want to diminish this happiness, so they continue to do what has made them happy to this point. That includes keeping in touch every few days and seeing each other occasionally. This could be once a week, twice a week, once every two weeks, or even once a month. The exact time spent together does not matter because they know that they will stay in touch, see other again, miss each other because they do not spend too much time together, and stay happy together.

Lisa is still thrilled with Joe at home during this time that she occasionally sees Brett. Joe and Brett do not have a problem with Lisa's situation because they see her happy all the time, and they each enjoy a positive relationship with her. For the first time in her life, Lisa has discovered true polyamory, and she is very happy with it. She loves both Joe and Brett and fully enjoys time with both. She and Brett still categorize her relationship with Joe as the primary relationship, and they don't worry about that because Brett and Lisa are happy together. Lisa and Joe know that Lisa is seeing other people, and they don't worry about that because they still have a great life together.

Once work settles down again for Joe, and he has his health and finances in order, he resumes seeing other people at times. Just like the standard dating world, his experiences are a random mix, but he develops some close relations as well.

This alternative relationship style continues for many years, with both Joe and Lisa staying respectful to each other, while also seeing other people occasionally. They found that seeing other people within this alternative relationship style made them appreciate certain qualities in certain people, including each other. Joe and Lisa found that you notice personality traits in people when they are involved in alternative situations that you would not have seen in standard situations. They like what they have learned from this and continue happily living the polyamory lifestyle together.

Society says to have as many friends as you want, have whatever job you want, practice or don't practice any religion you want, vote for who you want, and basically do anything that you legally want in this country, including being intimate with whoever you want, UNLESS…you are in a romantic relationship with someone. Two people in a romantic relationship should only be intimate with each other per society's standards, and neither should associate with anyone else that they could potentially have any sign of intimacy with because that would be a threat to the couple's connection.

If a heterosexual male in a relationship has lunch with a different girl for example, that would be questioned because this lunch would often be viewed as potentially deceitful, and thus a threat to the couple's monogamous agreement. Some would say this lunch is leading to other things, otherwise he wouldn't be there. It might be, it might not be. If he had lunch with a male friend, that wouldn't be perceived as leading to anything else though. Just because his lunch is with a female, it is automatically leading to something? What if two people just genuinely enjoyed each other's company, share laughs, have other interests in common, and genuinely enjoy seeing each other?

He already has a good connection with his girlfriend at home, why does he need to go see another girl, you say? He has a great connection with his best male friend, but he sees other friends at times too. Different people bring different connections in our lives, and this adds to the love in our lives. Maximize this love, don't minimize it by limiting yourself from who you see. If you have a great connection with someone, but this person is opposite sex, does this mean you cannot see this person once you are in a relationship? If nothing is being hidden from your partner, there should be no problems. If your partner does not want you to see this person because he or she feels threatened by that person, the real question might be the actual connection between you and your partner.

Provided the connection between you and your partner is strong, another person should not feel like a threat, and this should be clear to your partner. Someone from the opposite sex automatically serving as a threat to the relationship could mean that the relationship might be fragile. More communication may be needed, more trust established, or both. If other people that you see potentially involves intimate activities, then that should be discussed with your partner as well. Many people choose not to discuss it because they know their partner will not agree to it. They then act deceitfully and cheat. One must question why this cheating happened though. First off is because the partner did not, or would not agree to you being intimate with anyone else. You accepted that in the beginning when things were new and exciting, but now after a few years, you want those new and exciting feelings with someone else again. She isn't going for it because she feels threatened, or the thought of you naked with another girl makes her sick? Why is that? What is the real threat there? Does she fear that would change things between you two? Because you two are a couple, it now forbids you to be intimate with anyone else in the world?

To be fair, both sides agree to this monogamous behavior, so the fairness isn't coming into question, the reasoning behind it is. Why do people in monogamous relationships limit themselves from seeing certain people? Because that is what we grew up knowing from our family, Hollywood, and most everything in our world. As far as we know, we date people that we are interested in, and eventually we are supposed to marry our "soulmate", or at least settle down with one person. People follow this pattern, and it has been ingrained in our heads that if you truly love someone, then you become a monogamous couple and eventually marry. This is contrary to the fact that the institution of marriage was not originated for love at ALL.

MARRIAGE…a modern anachronism

From a very young age, children of all genders are told that the ideal way of living is that you grow up, find a partner and marry them. You will stay married to this person for the rest of your life, "forsaking all others". You will buy a house together, have children, etc. It's such a prevalent philosophy that an entire multi-million industry has grown around it. An enormous amount of dollars is spent each year on rings, dresses, flowers, food, photographers and so forth to celebrate this philosophy. Both partners say, "I do" and seal their union that, theoretically, lasts for the rest of their adult lives.

It may come as no surprise that it was the Catholic Church that championed the idea of monogamy in marriage. Between the 6th and 9th centuries, the church's battle for power over the power bases and royalty of Europe was won…by the church. They abolished the idea that kings could have more than one wife, and monogamy become the norm.

For hundreds of years, marriage was used to cement alliances. Love was rarely involved. It was about cementing alliances, exchanging of property/wealth and expanding the workforce necessary to work the land for the common people married. These reasons for marriage were so prevalent that in some cultures, children were married to the "spirit" of a dead child. To retain property and ensure the expansion of a family's workforce, marriage within families was common.

Marriage between the rich and royal was even more of a transaction. Partners rarely met each other before the wedding, and love was not a factor. Continuing the royal line/house was one of the prime aims of marriage, thus ensuring the continuation of dynastic families. Royalty married power bases, not lovers. It was especially common for kings to take outside partners, less so for queens, but it occurred with reasonable frequency. Marriage was simply a way to secure wealth, position and power. If love was the result, fine, but if not, there was little either party could do.

It was only about 250 years ago that the modern concept of love, romance and marriage became prevalent among all classes. Before this point, romantic love between partners was not looked upon favorably…actually, it was seen as more of a sickness of the mind. People went crazy when they were "in love", doing ridiculous things (example: Paris kidnapping Helen of Troy and starting an entire war over love/lust). Marriage was meant for baby making and cementing alliances. But at some point, during the Industrial Age, the idea of being romantically in love with your partner started to gain ground. All the questionable behaviors that people did to show their love for someone else became completely acceptable. Stories like Shakespeare's "Romeo and Juliet" were seen as romantic tragedies as opposed to cautionary tales about the foolishness of romantic love (like they were originally written as).

As people moved from making a living through agriculture to cities where paid jobs secured peoples economic situations, the idea of romantic love and sexual desire entered marriage (although to be honest, it was likely to be lust as opposed to love). It should be noted that the sexual desire was on the side of the male. It was a popular opinion that "respectable women" didn't have sexual urges at all. Neither did they have any rights to property or wealth. Marriage was the only way to secure some kind of future that kept them from being destitute spinsters.

It was after the World Wars and other hardships of the first half of the 20th century that the idea of romantic, monogamous love really became popularized. We can thank Hollywood and the American film industry for this. They popularized the idea of the ideal mate, and the fairy tale ideal of finding "the one" became accepted as desirable.

The modern reality is quite different. Romantic love and living happily ever after is really the biggest modern myth and con of the modern era. If you asked most married people why they married today, and they would often respond with "because we loved each other". So instead of staying together by choice, it has become a common belief that to show true love, couples need to sign a contract involving the government, and have a big, expensive ceremony, showing their friends and family this true commitment. People get swept up in the concept of romantic love, and they believe that everything will always be perfect, rose colored and loving.

What does marriage truly do for you though? Two people that truly love each other will stay together, whether or not they are married. They don't need a piece of paper to keep them together. They stay together by choice. Some would argue that married people can stay together by choice too. While true sometimes, how many marriages are kept together by love alone? Couples staying together *without* a marriage license are staying together 100% by choice. If one of them wanted to leave tomorrow, he or she could, with the only consequences being personal ones. People that are married have other things to consider if they want to split, and that involves the government, money, and many legal concerns, besides all the personal consequences. Not all marriages stay together because of love. There are life consequences to consider, and the added difficulty of relationship changes now that the law has been involved. The law is involved often, considering that about half of marriages currently end in divorce. Most of those divorces are not agreeable ones either, with each partner doing their best to harm their former partner. Houses are sold, assets are split, payments are made and finally both partners are free and many times bitter.

When asked why a marriage split, often partners will say "we just grew apart". This is not surprising. People change as they grow older. Some change for the better, some for the worse, but change happens. What was important when you were young often becomes trivial later in life. New interests come up that draw partners apart, or things that were endearing at first become unendurable as one gets older. Eventually the changes can create an unbridgeable gulf that neither partner wants to address. What was once a tight partnership, descends into roommate-like indifference, often accompanied by sexless months that become years. One partner decides they want more, and divorce is the result.

Sarah had been married to Glenn for 5 years, and things were stable in the beginning. Over the years, Glenn had slowly begun spending an increasing amount of time with work though. This took away from the time he had with Sarah and their 3-year-old daughter, Jessica. Things were ok financially at home because Glenn was doing very well for himself at work. The time he committed to work began to significantly impact the time he had available for his family. Sarah and Glenn discussed this, and while Glenn said that this time restraint would not last forever, it never seemed to change. Sarah did most of the parenting, raising Jess, but that did not leave much time for herself. She missed seeing her friends as much as she had before, and she missed the time spent, as well as the intimate times that she and Glenn used to have. Those were mostly non-existent now.

Instead of sitting around and being miserable though, Sarah talked about these things to her friends, the few times she saw them, and tried to talk to Glenn, to let him know her feelings. Glenn listened to her feelings, and tried to console her, but nothing changed as far as his time spent with work. Seeing all of this and knowing how Sarah felt, one of her friends mentioned the possibility of opening up the marriage, so Sarah could have some of her time with others, and maybe Glenn would then have more time with Jess. Maybe Glenn would even give it more of a priority to spend time with Sarah once he thought about her with another man occasionally.

Sarah brought up the open relationship possibility to Glenn, mentioning that maybe each of them seeing other people at times would make their time apart easier, and help them out overall, making their bond stronger. Glenn was traditional though, and all he had ever known and considered was monogamous marriages, so he did not even give Sarah's proposition a second thought. He would rather keep things how they are with him making the money, and Sarah doing most of the raising of their daughter Jess. This did not surprise Sarah because she knew Glenn as traditional, but it still upset her that he did not at least even consider it as an alternative solution to help her happiness. He wanted Sarah happy, but happy by what he thought was the appropriate way. Sarah listened to this, and while she was hurt by his replies, she agreed to not push the open relationship idea.

Because nothing changed, things went back to how they were with Glenn working all the time, and Sarah raising Jess, while being unhappy and increasingly lonely. Finally, after a few more months of the same routine, Sarah put herself online, looking for companionship, but also for some hot sex. She was hesitant to do this at first, but after years of nothing changing, and her husband doing nothing to change it, she finally looked out for herself and tried to experience happy times again. Sarah met a few people online, had some good dates with them, and eventually had some passionate intimate times with them. Even though she knew that she was being deceitful doing this, it filled a big void in her life that her husband did not seem to want to fill anymore, and she started to get happy again. After doing this for six months, she met someone that she really connected to. She was honest with him about her situation, and this new guy understood. He enjoyed seeing Sarah, and enjoyed everything they did together, from the laughing to the hot sex. Sarah began exclusively seeing this guy because they were having such great times together, and considering Jess at home, she did not have much time for other guys. Sarah and Aaron dated for a while, and Sarah was very happy during this time.

The point of Sarah's story was that she did not want to be deceitful to her husband Glenn. She tried to make things work in standard ways, and when that changed nothing, she tried alternative solutions. Glenn was not going for anything alternative, so she took things into her own hands. She loved herself for a change, instead of sacrificing and not being happy. What other solutions did she have? Divorce? They had a 3-year-old daughter, and she had been out of the working field for years since the marriage started. Yes, she could get back to work if they got divorced, but that would be a significantly harder lifestyle for Jess and her. She considered it, but ultimately did not want to change Jess' lifestyle, or increase her time away from the limited time she saw her father. So, Sarah started cheating on Glenn. She did not enjoy being deceitful at first, but when she saw how much happiness it gave her to fill the void in her life, and while questioning how little Glenn would have cared if he found out anyway, she became more comfortable with it.

How could this situation have been different? Obviously, Glenn could have paid more attention to his wife and daughter, but we don't know Glenn's situation at work. What if that wasn't really possible? What if he needed to do what he was doing just to keep the job? If he wanted to move up to a certain level in the company, this could have been more of a priority than extra time with his wife and child. We don't know what Glenn's situation was, we just know Sarah's increasing unhappiness. What if Glenn himself was cheating at times and occasionally seeing other women? Sarah did not think that he was, but considering how often he was away for work, she could not truly know.

If Glenn had just opened his mind when Sarah mentioned the open relationship idea, a lot of things could have been smoother. Sarah would not have to be deceitful for her happiness, Glenn might have made it more of a priority to see his wife and child more, and if he was in fact cheating on Sarah at all, he could see other women without being deceitful about it. Everyone would agree and be on the same page. He did not see it that way. He did not want the thought going through his traditional brain of his wife out with anyone else. Whether or not he was already doing this did not cross his mind. He simply and selfishly did not want her seeing other people, end of story.

Sarah and Glenn's situation and reasoning are common in marriages today, with many couples not even considering alternative solutions. Alternative solutions do not work for everyone, but if you have a strong connection with someone, just about anything can work, so remain open-minded.

What about when the inevitable "spark went out" happens? This is a common reason given for a marriage ending, and one which non-monogamy is situated to ease, as we will see in this next scenario.

Bill and Stacy met in high school. She was a senior and he a junior. They started going out at the beginning of Bill's junior year. It was the first serious relationship for both of them. They grew very close and fell in love. Stacy graduated and went to a local school so she could be close to Bill during his senior year. They saw each other as often as her study schedule allowed. Both were completely faithful to one another. When Bill graduated from high school, he joined Stacy at the local college, and the relationship continued. When Stacy graduated, they got married.

About 5 years into the marriage, Bill realized something. He loved Stacy very much, but he was bored...bored with his life and bored with the physical relationship they had. Having been with Stacy since he was 16 years old, he had never explored other sexual relationships, or his own sexual needs. He wanted to explore relationships with other women. He did not want to cheat on Stacy - although their relationship was essentially sexless. They had become such good friends over the years that he did not want to do anything that could be viewed as betraying that friendship. Just as importantly, he knew that neither of them could survive financially on their own. They both still had significant debt from college, and they had purchased a house about a year after being married. Bill felt suffocated and trapped, but felt he owed it to Stacy to discuss his problems with her.

One evening, he sat down with Stacy, and was very open about where his head was. Bill explained that he loved her very much, but physically he needed more. He told her about his desire to have relationships with other women. He ended his side of the conversation by saying that he felt trapped and did not want to do anything that would hurt Stacy, but he truly needed more.

Stacy was silent for a few moments and then did something that completely surprised Bill. She reached out and hugged him and started talking. Her words mirrored Bill's. She loved him, but physically was not interested in sex with him anymore. She also looked at other men and wanting to explore other relationships. She said she knew that financially they were not in a good place to end their marriage. Stacy reiterated how much she valued Bill as a close friend.

These revelations from both partners led to a discussion about the idea of opening their marriage. They agreed to do some reading on the concept of open marriages and discuss it further. After a great deal of reading and discussion, Stacy and Bill created a set of outside relationship guidelines to start. Over time, they adjusted their guidelines to allow both of them as much freedom as possible. Their explorations into other relationships actually changed their physical relationship. Although they still rarely had sex with each other, both could pursue other relationships while remaining close friends.

Both Stacy and Bill credit each other's willingness to sit and discuss what they were thinking and respecting each other enough to open their marriage rather than cheat. Allowing each other to explore relationships with others under guidelines agreed to by both kept their marriage from ending in divorce. Every 6 months, they review their current relationship rules, and if necessary, change them to ensure that both partners remain happy in their current situation. Although they both say they have no current plans to end the marriage, it could happen in the future. If it did, both agree that it would be an amiable and easy parting.

The spark that so many speak of is based on chemical processes that go on in the brain - sometimes called the dopamine effect. New Relationship Energy (NRE) is caused by this effect. Dopamine is a neurotransmitter - a chemical released by nerve cells that play a role in the excitement that comes with meeting a new person and starting a new relationship. The brain becomes excited by the idea of a new person and anticipates spending time with that person. Dopamine is also related to the same feeling drug addicts get when they take cocaine. Cocaine maintains dopamine signaling for longer than usual, giving users their "high". This same dopamine pathway lights up when we are attracted to another human being.

The dopamine effect is dizzying and a little addictive. New couples will spend time together constantly to keep the high going. They essentially become addicted to each other (initially at least). The desire to be together is driven by the need to feel that dopamine fueled high. Inhibitions are lowered and often the sex is amazing, far beyond what they would normally experience. There is nothing wrong with enjoying this high. The problems come when couples become wrapped up in the high and make decisions that will affect their futures while the dopamine high is still in effect. Eventually the high dissipates. What was once new and anticipated becomes routine. The release of dopamine becomes less and less until its effect is negligible. The "spark", i.e. the dopamine high, is gone.

Our desire to experience that pleasurable anticipation and excitement that accompanies the dopamine effect, coupled with boredom in a partner leads to cheating. Besides experiencing the dopamine effect, cheating often brings an adrenaline high. Sneaking around, communicating surreptitiously, meeting the new person on the sly is a rush to many people, a rush on par with bungee jumping or any other dangerous activity. It can be just as addictive as alcohol. Couple that with the exciting anticipatory rush of dopamine, and cheating becomes not just a means to sexual release, but a rush on other levels as well.

There are countless articles and books and advice about how to bring the spark back to your marriage, but the fact is, it's almost impossible. No amount of role play, or toys, or different sexual positions can counteract the fact that the person you are having sex with is the same person you have had sex with many, many times. Dopamine, or that "spark", is triggered by anticipating a new and exciting experience. It is extraordinarily difficult, virtually impossible, to create a sexual experience with a long-term partner that will stimulate the production of enough dopamine to "bring back the spark".

Unless…

Unless a reason is created to anticipate sex with that partner. This is where the open marriage/relationship paradigm can actually enhance a long-standing monogamous partnership.

When both partners see other people, they are opening themselves to new experiences and new connections. The neural pathways in the brain that are used by dopamine are re-stimulated as time spent with different people is anticipated. Although there is no definite supporting research, it is possible that the stimulation of the dopamine effect can carry over into the existing primary partnership. At the very least, the ability to experience the dopamine effect freely can allow a marriage to remain strong and amiable, as with Stacy and Bill.

Let's return to Stacy and Bill for a moment. One thing they credited with allowing them to keep their marriage together was reviewing the rules for their open marriage every 6 months. This self-evaluation and review, or "state of their union" discussion of a relationship is an excellent idea for all partnerships, marriage and otherwise. By sitting down and taking part in an open and honest conversation about the relationship, both parties would discuss problems and perhaps avert them (problems like cheating, for example). It also gives couples the opportunity to share what they are enjoying about a relationship–which is just as important as what may need improvement.

But let's take it a step further…or rather several steps further. To get married, a couple must go to the local government and apply for a license (nothing says "I love you" like getting the government involved in your relationship). When you receive a driver's license, or nursing license, or medical license or really any other license, it is subject to being renewed every so many years. What if marriage licenses were the same way? Say a couple decides to get married. Before they are granted a license, they sit down and hash out a 5-year plan that both parties agree to - essentially a short-term prenuptial contract. At the end of that five years, the couple would need to apply to renew their license, which would involve another relationship review and updating of the marriage contract. If the couple feels they want to continue the marriage, they renew their license. If not, they simply honor the term of the original contract (including providing for and co-parenting any children), and go their own ways, without acrimony or bitterness. Divorce would pretty much cease to exist. The likelihood of cheating would drop as well since each partner would know that the term of the marriage was finite, and they could walk away at the end of the license term. Communication between partners would, of necessity, have to be more open, honest and frequent between partners.

But what if…what if…marriage was not the relationship goal in the first place? What if, instead of following the narrative that society has laid out for us, and that we are catechized in from a young age, we step off that path and follow an entirely different relationship goal? Instead of continuing on with what is a societal expectation imprinted on us, we stopped and questioned why exactly we were choosing to get married? Ask questions like "What exactly can marriage offer us that a strong, committed long term relationship isn't already giving us?" What are the real benefits to entering a long-term business contract versus staying together because you are both committed to staying? And really…what is wrong with just having a long-term relationship where both parties stay because they want to versus staying because a business contract makes it difficult for them to leave?

Robert and Wendy had been married for 20 years. It was not a harmonious marriage. In fact, it had been one rife with arguments, accusations of cheating and actual cheating. Wendy had been caught cheating more than once early in the marriage. After being caught, she claims she never cheated again. However, she became controlling and verbally abusive of Robert, doing her best to ensure that he felt that she was the best he could ever do, in terms of a partner.

Robert, on the other hand, had cheated multiples times from the time of engagement on. As the years went in their marriage, his main reason for cheating was the "spark going out" and the adrenaline rush he got from cheating on his spouse. He had many outside affairs, and when caught (as he was several times), he would throw all the blame on the other person, convincing Wendy that he was not at fault, which would bring them closer together for a while.

Clearly neither Robert nor Wendy was capable of open and honest communication. When asked, Robert claimed he had brought up the idea of an open marriage, but Wendy's response was so opposed and verbally abusive, that he dropped that conversation immediately and never mentioned it again. Robert also said that he knew right from the beginning, when they became engaged, he knew he was incapable of being faithful/monogamous. Rather than discuss that at the beginning of the relationship, he tried (unsuccessfully) to be monogamous. When that didn't work, he chose to cheat - both to satisfy his need for other sexual partners, but later because he became addicted to the adrenaline rush of cheating. Instead, he used cheating as a way to 'bring the spark back', creating a series of partners who were resentful at having been used as an alternative to marriage therapy and to "put the spark" back, not the marriage.

Clearly there were many problems with this marriage...the primary one being one partner (Robert) was in no way committed to monogamy. Imagine if this couple could have an open and honest conversation about the problems in their marriage, the primary one being a loss of interest in each other. Imagine if, instead of cheating and verbal abuse, they communicated their need to see other people, and then followed through on it. Or even better, imagine if they had addressed Robert's inability to be monogamous right from the start. It would have allowed them to either change the parameters of their marriage to include the concept of open/polyamory or not get married to start with.

Jeanne has never been married, and she answered a few questions on this topic.

The common belief still prevalent today is that true love ultimately leads to marriage.

What is your view on the institution of marriage?

I believe the CONCEPT of marriage is nice...together forever, 'til death do us part, raising a family, sharing a life, growing old together, etc... But I believe two people can share this life together without a signed legal document. A lasting relationship, in general, is only as strong as the commitment between the couple-- a piece of paper does not strengthen a relationship. I believe many marriages fail because they stop trying so hard to impress each other once they get married, and rely solely on this signed legal document to keep them together. Marriage is their "destination" when actually it should be their "beginning"... they forget all about their life journey together, they become lazy, and take each other for granted. They have this signed legal document that states they have to stay together "for better or for worse", and THAT'S what makes them lazy. I don't believe this happens to ALL marriages. A lot of marriages actually work...but it's the couple who makes it work, not a piece of paper. A couple that WANTS to be together WILL be together, and they will achieve this through their commitment to each other...and that has NOTHING to do with a signed legal document.

In the years that you have been dating, why have you never gotten married before?

I've never gotten married by choice...although marriage is not something I've ever wanted; I do 100% believe in committed relationships.

Do you see any benefits in marriage? Any drawbacks in marriage?

I know people who DID benefit from getting married, but it had less to do with love, and more to do with getting health coverage for their partner's kids...some people also get married for citizenship.

A drawback would be couples feeling "trapped" in a marriage because of the kids involved, or financial burdens...sometimes it's just easier (financially) to stay married.... I know many people in this situation.

Do you know people that have had bad marriages?

I know people who have bad marriages...and I also know people who are happily married. And it all boils down to the couple. If you want something bad enough, you work hard to keep it…if you don't, you part ways and move on. And I believe the fate of the relationship should be between the couple, NOT a piece of paper.

To provide a perspective from someone who has been married for over 11 years, Kimberly answered some questions on marriage.

Even though the institution of marriage was NOT originally formed with love in mind, the common belief became, and is still mostly prevalent today, that true love ultimately leads to marriage. As a married person, what is your current view on marriage?

If a couple chooses to "solidify" their relationship with marriage, that's their prerogative. There are many who believe that marriage is the only way in or out. There are many who believe that marriage is nonsense. Each is entitled to their own beliefs and choices. There are pros and cons to both paths. The problem, I feel, is that we as a society are wildly under-educated on the topic. Today, as a married person for 11 years to someone I do truly love, I see the union as a lock-down; pressure to make it work no matter what; sharing everything on god's green earth with that one and only person. It's suffocating. Of course, there are many more factors that contribute to a marriage working or not. But, in a nutshell, there it is.

Is your current view of marriage different from your original views of marriage when you first were married? If your views are different at all, what caused these changes?

My view on marriage has changed a great deal over the years. Starting off as the belief that we are supposed to find "THE ONE", then date for the appropriate time, get married, buy a house, have children, and live happily ever after...or bullshit along those lines. These are the steps that most of us are programmed to believe, that lead to lifelong happiness. I have two happily married parents that have been together for over 40 years. Why would I believe anything different should exist? I've been with my husband for over 15 (4 years before the marriage). About 7 years into the relationship, I started to feel very differently about marriage. I began to feel trapped...like there should be more (or maybe less) to this relationship. But also, I felt like there was no way out because we have children together and a home and debt, etc. We have lost our partnership because of it. I started to research, as well as read and talk to friends and loved ones, and found that SO MANY feel the same way...that there is not just one person for each of us, that we can love more than one person at a time, that we don't need marriage to do it, that we don't need rings or priests, or a certificate to prove our 'forever' with a person, and most importantly, the idea that there is no way that one single person can possibly give us everything that we need in life and in a relationship. Most of us have more than 1 friend. Each friend is important to us for different reasons. We get different things out of different friendships. How can we expect our love life to be any different? If I were to do it again, it would look much different now. I still believe in the union of marriage because I think for many, the idea of the symbolic process still holds true to them. But I've realized, a commitment has nothing to do with marriage. I'm still learning, and observing and have so much more to learn on the subject, and about myself, but I can say that the realizations I've had about societies' take on marriage vs. the reality, has been freeing to say the least.

Do you see any benefits in marriage? Any drawbacks in marriage? If so, what?

I think there are a lot of benefits in a marriage...if there is a true partnership, willingness to share a life together, consistent communication, genuine respect and acceptance, and the ability to be flexible and compromise. But then again...a happy couple need not be married to have these qualities

What is your experience with non-monogamous relationships?

I began having relationships outside of my marriage a few years ago. Some have been with other married individuals and some not. Some agreeing with the idea that marriage is for the birds, and others being consumed with guilt because it is "breaking the rules" of marriage. Either way, the idea of a non-monogamous relationship is something that I never thought I'd consider until having my "extra-marital" experiences.

30

What is the perfect relationship set-up to you as far as exclusive/non-exclusive, living together/living apart, future goals, serious/casual?

It's become most important to me to have an open mind regarding relationships. It's a constant work in progress. There are so many factors that contribute to a happy relationship and each depends on the couple. If we are talking about a true love relationship with one person... Living with another person; but need to be alone and take space for myself. A non-exclusive relationship; but still want to feel loved. A serious relationship; but need the free time to be with friends, family, and my work.

A favorite quote shared by a favorite person..."There are many paths to happiness, peace, and contentment, and they all look different. If your actions are safe, healthy, positive, and not causing harm, you get the privilege of creating and owning your path to happiness."

CHEATING….

Studies have shown that people who cheat on their partners do so for a variety of reasons. There is no denying that the concept of cheating itself is wrong because it is a deceitful breach of an agreement. The reasons cheating happens could point out alternatives to avoid this deceitful behavior. One reason people cheat is because they give in to an attraction to another person.

You may have an interest in a certain someone, or certain people, but you do not pursue them because you are in an exclusive relationship and you don't want to break that agreement. This is not that challenging in the beginning of a new relationship because the new relationship is still exciting, and that consumes most of the focus. This new relationship excitement lasting forever is unlikely though. You have a strong connection with your partner, but you have also restricted yourself from other people for a while, despite the occasional temptation. Some people continue to honor their exclusive agreement, and while this is honorable, it opens up the possibility of resentment due to the biological fact that humans are not meant to be monogamous. Another avenue people choose in these situations is cheating. While cheating satisfies the temptation with another person urge, it breaks the initial exclusive agreement made with the partner.

What is the solution to this predicament? There are various possible solutions, including opening up the relationship as one of them. Since open relationships are still not common in society, many people do not know what open relationships entail. Just like any relationship, open relationships can be handled in many ways. One style of opening up relationships consists of the partners staying together as primary partners, but also occasionally seeing other people. This satisfies the occasional urge with other people, while not disrupting the strong connection that you two already have (and potentially have built up for a while).

There are many other styles of opening the relationship, including one of you seeing others, one of you not, both of you seeing other couples, both of you having significant others also, etc. The main point of any open relationship formation, just in a standard relationship setup is that both sides need to agree. Even though it differs from standard monogamous arrangements because other people are involved, it is important to remember how crucial it is to follow established agreements, just like in standard relationships (maybe even more so because other people are involved).

Seeing other people is cheating in a monogamous relationship, but breaking an agreement in an open relationship is "cheating" as well. Did you both agree to see other people, as long as neither of you brings any of them to your home? That agreement needs to be followed. If it is broken, and either of you bring someone else home, then that is cheating the agreement and being deceitful. Just because you both agreed to see other people, does not mean that all rules go out the window and respect is gone. You need to be more respectful now because there are more people involved. You not only need to be respectful of whatever agreements that you made with your primary partner, but you also need to be respectful with anyone you see.

A common response when opening a relationship is mentioned as an option by people these days is "my partner won't go for that". This is often true because when a partner is presented with this option, many do not even actually think about it because their head is immediately clouded with negative perceptions about a subject that most people know very little about. Many just brush off open relationships as swinging, or get worried that the partner would leave them for another person. Those views are not what open relationships are about though.

Rick and Sally had been together for 5 years, and while both had occasionally had the urge for others during their time together, they had been exclusive because that was all they really knew how to be in romantic relationships. Rick had told his friends about one of his co-workers that he was very attracted to, but had resisted pursuing because of his relationship with Sally. When one of his friends suggested opening up the relationship so he could pursue this co-worker without doing anything wrong, Rick shook his head, blurting out "No, I don't want Sally fucking other dudes!", and immediately dismissed the concept.

Months went by, and he couldn't resist holding back from going after the co-worker, so he started flirting with her, she was into him, and they went out for drinks after work a few times. One time out, one of Sally's friends was at the bar they were at, and when Sally found out about this, she asked Rick about it. Rick came clean and admitted to Sally that he slept with the co-worker, and despite apologizing over and over for this, Sally was hurt. She was not hurt that he slept with someone else, but hurt over the deceit of it. He had hidden it from her, so who knows what else he would hide.

When she gathered her thoughts, she sat down and talked freely to Rick. She acknowledged that they both have had temptations with others at times, yet supposedly had done nothing about that. She mentioned that she was ok with opening the relationship up so they could satisfy this desire to see others at times while staying together. Unfortunately, Rick did not think about the benefits this arrangement would have for their relationship, and he kept focusing on Sally with other guys. He disregarded the fact that he had desires for others at times, and would rather cheat and be deceitful to their exclusive agreement (like he already had done) than think about Sally with other guys.

After forgiving him for cheating, trying to be patient in explaining the logical benefits of opening the relationship, Sally still could not get Rick to agree on opening the relationship. Because he was insistent on holding on to the mirage that both of them being exclusive to each other was the best thing, even with his outside desires still going on, Sally knew Rick would not change. Because Rick was steadfast in his ways, and would not open his mind to other possibilities, Sally ended things with Rick. She reiterated her point to him that she was not ending things because he slept with someone else. She ended things because he was deceitful to her, and because he did not want the same opportunities for her that he had. Having concluded that, she told him that he did not truly care about her, and she moved on.

Think Rick should have agreed to Sally's open relationship suggestion? Some would say he should, others no. Rick was still hanging on to the concept that he would rather take a chance and be deceitful than be open and honest, allowing his girlfriend to occasionally see other men. Logistically, he should agree to opening the relationship because then he can satisfy his desire to see others while breaking no agreements.

Logic does not apply 100% in relationships though, and emotion comes into play. He let his emotions decide for him and his unfair emotions were focused on Sally with other guys. He was not confident enough in himself to think that she would not leave him for someone else, so he tried to prohibit that possibility from even happening. This emotion ignored the fact that he still had temptations to be with other girls and also ignored being fair with Sally. She saw that he could not separate these emotional thoughts and think rationally about the situation, so she justifiably ended things.

Essentially, cheating is a completely avoidable thing if couples would agree to open, honest, transparent conversations combined with relationship reviews. If both parties can agree to keep an open mind, and both can get past reacting out of jealousy instead of thinking logically about the situation, an open relationship in various forms can prevent cheating. Both partners have the chance to enjoy the dopamine effect regularly, which can translate to keeping a relationship solid. Additionally, time spent with other people can allow the original couple to better appreciate their existing partner. Being "open to open" can help relationships (whether they are long term committed or actual marriages) survive in a world where differing priorities and a loss of interest are so prevalent as reasons for splitting.

COMMUNICATION NEEDS

Many people don't even consider open relationships as a realistic possibility for them. Many of the ones that do, think about it, don't take any actions, or even talk about it with their partner. Then there are the couples who actually talk about it and try it. Even if a couple decides that it is not for them, at least the subject can be discussed if either of them are curious about this relationship style. If you cannot talk about any topic with the person that you are in a long-term relationship with, then who can you freely talk to about anything and everything with? Some people do not even bring up opening the relationship because of a hunch what the partner's response would be. Then there is the possible discomfort about raising the topic in the first place. This is an understandable precaution. If opening the relationship is on a person's mind regularly, it is not healthy to keep that held in forever, so the subject should be discussed. If opening the relationship is just a random fantasy, casually bringing it up to your partner might not hurt either to see his or her initial reaction. It is not a common subject discussed amongst traditional couples, so casually talking about it sometime might shed some light on possibilities.

One reason people hesitate to open relationships is the fear of "losing" your partner to someone else. The mentality is that if your partner is seeing other people besides you, there is a greater chance that he or she drifts to someone else. This ignores the fact that if your partner would leave you for someone else, it would most likely happen regardless of the relationship style. If the connection between you and your partner is solid, your relationship style (monogamous or not) will not determine either partner leaving the other. Think about it. If a connection is not strong between a pair in a standard monogamous relationship, either partner is just as likely to leave the other. The point here is to not have a concern about your partner straying off because of the relationship style. If you were worried about your partner leaving you for someone else, then there are different issues to deal with besides opening up the relationship in the first place.

Standard monogamous relationships limit the pair to only one sexual relationship, so that opens up a higher chance of infidelity and deceit. If one partner wants to be intimate with others, but their partner is not "allowing" that to happen, the only way for the other partner to satisfy these sexual needs is to be secretive about it. Without both partners coming to some agreement on all of their needs, there will be secrets. If a partner is not sexually or emotionally satisfied, this is an important communication matter. Relationships have dissolved because of this matter and holding it in because you think you know your partner's response is not a solution either. That leads to lying and cheating to satisfy your needs, and then you look like the corrupt person not holding up your end of the monogamous agreement. If your needs and desires were discussed ahead of time, even if your partner did not agree to it, at least you would not be deceitful. It all goes back to the simple fact that if your partner denies or dismisses your sexual or emotional needs, that person is not a person you that you will be happy with in a relationship.

Once you have these personal discussions with your partner, if one of you does not agree to one or more of the other's requests, instead of just immediately dismissing it, take a step back and talk about it more. Explore different options that could satisfy both of you. When a partner is not agreeing with one of your relationship suggestions, ask why. Get legitimate constructive answers. Don't just accept "because I don't want to" answers. Ask why, and what is he or she afraid of? What are the worst- and best-case scenarios if this change happened? Talk about any change calmly and listen to how the other feels. You want your needs satisfied, but you care about your partner, and you want that person's needs satisfied as well. Being open to alternatives–other than breaking up–should be important and discussed openly and completely.

When a couple is completely open and honest, they can acknowledge their own limits to what they can provide and share to keep their partner happy. We cannot be everything to someone else, no matter how close we are to that person. We are only one person, and this cannot completely satisfy another person's every need. Monogamy attempts to satisfy every desire of that person, and that is not possible. Allowing other people to satisfy some of these needs and desires of our partner should not be viewed hastily, but in a completely rational one.

NOT JUST ABOUT SEX

The hardest thing for those that do not engage in the poly/NM lifestyle to understand is how it is NOT just about sex. That is important enough to say again: NON-MONOGAMY AND POLYAMORY IS NOT JUST ABOUT SEX. Sex is normally a part of it, but it's NOT the only thing. Poly/NM is about making connections to other people in order to fill needs and desires. It is NOT just to sleep with a bunch of different people. Think about any standard relationship that you have had with someone. Were they all just about sex? Yes, certain relationships people have are just a sexual connection, but most are not just about that element. Some people have their friends with benefits, or have casually dated some in the past where sex was one of the highlights, but more often than not, sex is not the only component in the bulk of your past relationships.

Just like in standard monogamous relationships, intimacy can be a big component of an open relationship, but also similar to standard relationships, sex is not the only component in polyamorous relationships. Every person in this world is different, with certain people having similarities to you, and other people sharing different traits than you.

Think of it like you think of your platonic friends. Some friends of yours enjoy the same food and atmospheres as you do so you might generally go to the same restaurants and bars together. You might have other friends that you would never go to these locations with though, instead enjoying different activities with these other people. You might share an enjoyment of sports with some friends, discuss movies with others, have the same sense of humor with some, share music tastes with some, drinks with some, or a combination of those things. Regardless of how similar or different the experiences we have with those that we associate with, every platonic relationship that we have is different to some degree. It is the same with polyamorous relationships. Think of these simply as more friendships in your life. Many people don't see it that way because of the sexual element.

Some people think sex changes friendships. That could be the case with some people, but just like a lot of things in life, not the case with other people. Jim and Eileen might be intimate together, but that doesn't mean that they are intimate every time they get together. Sometimes they might just see each other to catchup and get a bite to eat together, sometimes they might watch a movie and relax together, while other times they might be sexual. Some of those things might happen, some might not.

It goes back to acknowledging that no matter how close two people are in a relationship, there are always different people in the world sharing certain qualities in common and offering different experiences for a person. Limiting yourself to only one person prevents you from different experiences with other people. Just because you see people outside a standard relationship doesn't mean that it is just for sex.

Will and Sandy had been married for 3 years and had a two-year-old boy together. They were both very busy between work, home, and Dave, their son. Sometimes they still did things together, like going out to dinner, taking Dave to places he enjoyed, or staying in with a movie. They both enjoyed time together, but were also very independent people, doing things on their own plenty too. Will and Sandy both took turns watching Dave when the other had to work late, or the other wanted to do something with a friend.

This seemed like a typical marriage to many on the outside, but the difference was that some of the friends that they saw when they went out were of the opposite sex. They married as a monogamous couple and enjoyed the first few years together in this fashion. They communicated very well with each other and talked about a lot of different things. One of them was the subject of seeing other people at times. There was nothing wrong between Will and Sandy, but the discussion had started because while Will and Sandy knew they were a great match for each other, they were confident enough in each other and trusted the other so they could comfortably talk about having interests in other people at times.

So, each of them occasionally went out and saw other people. Some of the other people were people they knew before their relationship, and some they met online from various dating apps. There are some polyamorous dating apps, but because the number of people on these apps was still lower than standard dating apps, they went on both types. This was challenging at times because most people they talked to were not interested in engaging with open relationships, typically because these other people knew nothing about this type of relationship.

It worked out in varying degrees with the people who gave it a chance though. New connections and friendships were made, exciting memories created, and an overall type of happiness brought to Will, Sandy, and the people they met. Will and Sandy remained a great couple at home, as well as developing some great connections with other people that they wouldn't have known if they had never opened up their relationship.

People were told the story of Will and Sandy, and there were various reactions ranging at both ends of the spectrum. One extreme group could not understand how Will and Sandy could still be a couple after seeing other people. The other mindset thought it was great that Will and Sandy opened their relationship, and felt that it made them even stronger as a couple because while seeing other people was nice, it reinforced how great their connection together was. Lastly there were those in the middle who remained open to the non-monogamous lifestyle, but still had some questions on certain details like the jealousy aspect, the time management in seeing other people, and how the other people would feel about seeing someone already in an existing relationship.

This all goes back to how strong the primary relationship is, in this case between Will and Sandy. Sandy had no problem acknowledging that Will was attracted to other girls, yet she also knew that this did not take away from how he felt about her. Knowing his feelings for her had not changed enabled her not to be jealous when Will occasionally went out and saw other girls.

Will knew that things were great between him and Sandy, so Sandy sporadically seeing other guys did not feel like a threat at all.

The relationships Will and Sandy had with other people were not necessarily sexual anyway, so in a lot of ways, it was simply more friends to hang out with. Their everyday lives together were no different and mixing experiences up in life was generally a good thing for their overall happiness. Will did not even think about it when she went on dates with other guys. He just wanted her to have fun, get home safe, and stay clean.

Many people are hesitant about involving themselves with someone who is already in an open relationship. The initial thought process when dating usually starts with "I want to find someone….". This person wanting to find someone hears about someone in an open relationship, and they immediately become reticent to it because the thought process is that the open relationship person already has someone, so they "wouldn't be there for me".

When having the goal of "finding someone" though, one must ask themselves to what degree do they want to find someone. Do you want to live with someone, see someone every day, see them once a week, go out to eat and drink with someone, have sex with someone, hang out and watch Netflix with someone, text buddy with someone, or something else? Having an idea what you want is important before you meet someone that you do not know. Many people may want the standard boyfriend/girlfriend relationship, and since that is still a large percentage of relationships, that common theme can be easy to search for. What about if your schedule only allows you to see someone once a week though? Between work, children, friends, home, and many other things in life, people only have so much free time, and some of this free time is for personal activities like exercise, hobbies, rest, etc.

An important aspect of loving yourself is making the time to do the things that you want to do, and that includes seeing other people. A busy divorced mom who is working and raising children does not have much free time. A father working two jobs to make ends meet, while still keeping active to stay in shape, only has so much time to keep a healthy social life. Many people for various reasons are busy with everyday life, but that does not mean that they should exclude everything from their life. If a person wants to enjoy a dating life, they should do so, regardless of how little, or how much free time they have.

Life changes all the time, so that "only free once a week" schedule of yours now might become "free twice a week" months down the road. Next year your life could differ greatly from what it is now, so don't think of things in terms of never or forever. If you see someone once a week, does it matter what that person does on those other six days? If you see someone once every two weeks, does it matter what that person does on the other 13 days? You might be in touch by text, phone, or email with a person regularly, and then see the person when you both are free. You enjoy each other's company, stay in touch, and both live your lives, regardless of what the other person does in their life. That is just one example of how an open relationship could work for people.

What if the people seeing each other wanted more? That is a possibility, and just like in a standard relationship where one person wants more, it can be discussed and managed together. We saw that Will and Sandy branched out to see other people after having dated for a few years. The other people they saw sometimes remained casual, sometimes a little more.

When a guy named Jeff started to get closer to Sandy after seeing her for a few months, he questioned whether he wanted to do this anymore. Jeff already knew about Will at home, and he was fine with that. He knew that Sandy sometimes saw other people besides him, and he was ok with that too. Sandy and Jeff were having a great time together though, and he simply wanted to talk about possibilities to help him fully grasp them. After talking things through, the thought process turned to them on a journey, not a destination. Sandy and Jeff weren't trying to commit to anything, they didn't "need" the other person, and they were not insecure about each other seeing other people. They sometimes just wanted more of the enjoyment they were having together. Whether it be just meeting for a drink, going out to dinner and a show, watching a movie, a hot night in bed, or basically anything with the other person, it was nice for them to talk about, and feel on the same page with each other.

Jeff knew how Sandy felt about Will at home and also knew that her feelings for Will did not take away from her feelings for him. Jeff and Sandy continued to live their lives while also enjoying their journey together. This was not always easy, but there are always times in every relationship where things can be difficult. How these challenging times are managed can say a lot about the people themselves, as well as how important they are to each other.

Just because Jeff and Sandy might be on a journey does not mean that Sandy and Will are not too. The unconscious bias is to think less of the journey that Will and Sandy are on (than if they were being monogamous) because they see other people, so they cannot be that strong of a connection. This thought occurs automatically to many people who view this type of situation because as humans, we don't normally see things as they are, we see things how WE are. The perception people have of Will and Sandy is initially influenced by anything the thinker has been through in life, and what the thinker is currently experiencing. How do you feel about Will and Sandy seeing other people? Now take a step back and think about how your perception is influenced by your experience, your surroundings, and your current situation.

Will and Sandy have been together for years, so they have been on a journey together for years. If Sandy and Will ever split, the natural thought would be that it was because of Sandy and Jeff. Sandy and Jeff do not affect their connection though. If Sandy and Will ever split, it will be because their journey ran its course.

FRIENDSHIPS VS. ROMANTIC RELATIONSHIPS

You commonly hear or talk about how the best romantic partners are best friends, right? This is important because if you are spending significant time with someone, you know you should be at least mutually compatible, and ideally, best friends. Your best friend relationship with your romantic partner differs from the relationship that you have with your platonic best friend though. Your platonic best friend would not restrict you from being intimate with anyone else, but in a monogamous relationship, your romantic best friend may restrict that.

The intimacy that you share with your romantic partner can make that partner seem significant in your life, and if you share other life activities with that person, such as living with them, then they become an important part of your life. Does that mean that they dictate your life though? This person should decide who you see and what you can and cannot do? Being respectful of this person's wishes differs from following orders, and we all should be respectful of people that we care about. Respect this person's wishes, but what if certain desires of this person do not coincide with what you believe in or want?

Where the relationship is going is often something that is discussed, with the infamous "what are you looking for?" question often asked in the beginning. Two people may often look for the same things, and these are usually discussed upfront to make sure both sides have an idea where the other one's head is at. What if one partner wanted to see other people besides this person? Many people want to categorize things, so they might say "she still wants to date", or "he wants to play the field still", or "they want to keep things casual", and immediately not take this couple as seriously as another couple that is exclusively dating each other. What if this couple were just as into each other as many exclusive couples (even more so than some of them), yet still wanted to see other people? Their connection should be taken less seriously?

Sherry and Chris met through an online dating app and hit it off well. They saw each other a few times, were interested in continuing that, so they kept seeing each other. Sherry and Chris knew they were both into each other, but at first, were having fun on their dates, and hadn't talked about any future possibilities yet. Sherry brought it up eventually, asking Chris if he had an idea what he wanted out of them yet. Chris wanted to keep seeing Sherry, but hadn't thought beyond that point so far.

Sherry was honest and told Chris that she was into him a lot and wanted to keep seeing him. She also mentioned that because she cared about him, she wanted to make sure that he was ok with her occasionally seeing others at times still. Chris had already developed a trust with her, and knew that if this ever presented any problems between the two, that she would be fair, and they would talk about it, so he said yeah, no problem. In his mind, Sherry occasionally seeing other people did not change the great connection those two had, and this enabled him to occasionally see other people as well. They both had this discussion, were glad that they were on the same page, and kept having a great time together.

Even though this continued for six months, Sherry's more traditional friend Amanda did not take her relationship with Chris as a serious one. Sherry saw other guys occasionally, but since she and Chris has developed such a strong friendship, she saw him more than anyone, and he had become her primary. While Sherry wasn't really into labels, to keep things simple, she started to call Chris her boyfriend when she described him to people, yet when Amanda heard Sherry call him that, she said "He's not your boyfriend. You two are just dating because you see other guys too." Sherry replied, "So he isn't my boyfriend, until I am exclusively seeing him and no one else?" Amanda immediately answered with "Yeah, how can he be your boyfriend when you date other guys? Unless you're cheating on him."

Instead of getting offended, Sherry knew that Amanda's brain was only thinking all that it ever knew, so she replied "Amanda, you can have a boyfriend or girlfriend, and also date other people at the same time. Hell, you can be married, and see other people concurrently. It is called an open relationship, or polyamory. It is just a different type of relationship structure than the standard monogamous setup. Neither one is right nor wrong. It is just important that both sides of the relationship agree with the structure and respect it."

This was hard for Amanda to believe at first, but she knew Sherry for a long time, and trusted Sherry to know what she was talking about, so she hesitantly accepted this information from Sherry, and then educated herself about relationship styles that are different from all that she had grown up knowing. Between reading and learning about open relationships, and seeing how pleased Sherry and Chris were together (now approaching two years together), Amanda came around to recognizing that this alternative relationship style worked for Chris and Sherry, and she legitimately thought of them as a happy "couple".

Sherry and Chris are an example of a few things. First off, they represent two people that are honestly happy together. Being happy together with no deceit involved is one of the most important things in a relationship, regardless of the relationship style.

If monogamy is important to you, make sure your partner is on the same page. If seeing other people is important to you, make sure you are on the same page with your partner as well. Just like it is important to mutually be on the same page in crucial topics like moving in together and having children, it is important to ensure that you both see eye to eye on the relationship structure itself. You wouldn't ignore discussing children with your partner if that was something important to you, so the details of the relationship structure should be discussed too. You want to see other people, but you don't think your partner would go for that? What if you wanted to have kids, and you knew your partner did not? You would still bring that important topic up, so the relationship structure should be discussed between you both too. Ideally, you both want the same thing, or at least will work together towards the same thing. If you don't, and cannot agree, one or both will not be fully happy in the relationship.

Loving yourself first includes living how you want to live. This is ideally done in mutual agreement with your partner. If it is not, then you generally should not be with that person. Some people think that sacrificing a little is not a big deal for those that we care about, and that is true, as long as these sacrifices do not interfere with your overall happiness. Know yourself, and what you want. If you want a monogamous relationship with this person, and your partner wants the same thing, perfect. If one of you generally enjoys seeing other people, like Sherry in the above scenario, but she gives that up because Chris wants monogamy, she might manage this happily for a little while, but ultimately, she will not be satisfied with the setup.

People sometimes sacrifice certain things in the beginning because the new relationship energy is so high that the sacrifices seem small compared to the overall greatness of things. That can be true in the relationship's beginning, but does not stay that way forever. What if Sherry and Chris had not agreed on the relationship structure of seeing other people? Would they have stopped seeing each other? What if Sherry sacrificed at first, and only saw Chris, then ultimately cheated on him to satisfy her desire to see others? That would be wrong and deceitful, yet that is often what people do. They either sacrifice, or ignore their desire to see other people in the beginning of a new relationship, and then later in the relationship, satisfy that urge by cheating. They are rightly viewed upon unfavorably for this deceitful action, when ultimately their root cause of this was because they gave into a relationship setup that was not something they wanted.

We know that good communication can be one of the strongest qualities in relationships, and part of this is discussing important aspects of the relationship. This includes whether either partner wants to be exclusive, still casually date, get more serious while still seeing others, or anything involving your time together. If the relationship is discussed and fully agreed upon for both sides, then the relationship at least has a solid foundation to build on. That is not saying there will be no problems. Stuff happens, but if any problems do surface, they most likely will be small, resolvable ones, because the overall foundation is strong. Start with the strong foundation, and build upon that, but have realistic expectations.

WHAT IS ETHICAL NON-MONAGAMY?

Ethical non-monogamy is an agreement between two people that while dating each other, either, or both of you can also date others. Most people would say "so you're just dating". Being non-monogamous and single may seem comparable, but it's not. First, when you say you are simply "dating", there is the expectation in society that you are in search of "the one". You are dating different people in succession and there is the expectation that eventually you will settle on a single person, stop dating all others, and relax into a comfortable, exclusive relationship. With non-monogamy, there is no intention of finding "the one". There can exist strong connections in non-monogamy, but never an exclusive connection, regardless of how close a connection with someone gets.

People are taxonomically classified as primates. Our nearest relatives are the great apes, specifically Bonobos. Very little other than a few mutated genes separate us from this species. If you look at the social structure of the Bonobo, you find that they are FAR from monogamous. In fact, they continually pair off with different members of their troop. There is little fighting over any kind of breeding rights, as they have no problem having sex with any member of the troop - there is no "ownership" of eligible females by a single male. Bonobos constantly enjoy sex for the sake of sex, as well as to produce offspring. Compared to their nearest great ape cousins, the Chimpanzee, their society is peaceful and far more egalitarian. But make no mistake, when they DO mate, bonobos are genetically driven to always seek the best possible mate AT THAT MOMENT to produce offspring with. Let's say that again… they are GENETICALLY DRIVEN to seek the best possible mate AT THAT MOMENT. In other words, they are in no way monogamous from year to year. They are always seeking the mate that is the best one for that time.

Why then, when dating, are we told we should seek a single mate that will be our partner for the rest of our lives? We are closely related to Bonobos and have the same genetically driven imperative to seek the best possible mate for the moment. The myth of monogamy drives this tale.

Every day you are a slightly different person than you were the day before. You've learned something, or experienced something that impacted you and makes you a different person. It doesn't have to be something soul shaking (although of course it could be), but you are a little different in some way. From day to day, those little changes aren't much, but taken in their totality over time, it equals a BIG difference. As you change and grow, so too will your needs - and I do mean ALL needs; social, mental, emotional and physical/sexual. Just because YOU are changing though, it doesn't mean that your mate has changed, or has changed in such a way as to still be compatible with you and your goals in life (which like everything else, will probably change).

You may realize you and your so-called life-partner have diverged to where you are maintaining a relationship that is little more than a friendship. Yet society says you cannot seek a mate that better suits you without divorcing your current mate. What if, for any number of reasons, you do not want to separate from your spouse, but all of your needs are not being met? Your option is to cheat on your spouse/partner.

Instead, what if you had a talk with your partner - an open and honest talk about the needs you both have - and agreed that you could see other people while staying together? You open a channel of communication that leads to productive and agreeable solutions which allow you stay together without creating resentment or hurt feelings. In other words, what if you allowed yourselves the chance to "go Bonobo" while still coming home to each other?

You might share your experiences with your partner (that is decided between you both), and know that they are happy because you are happy, and vice versa. Rather than hurting your relationship, this can actually strengthen it. That is what non-monogamous/open/poly relationships are all about; allowing your partner to love and be with others, and loving each other BECAUSE they see others (and so do you), rather than despite it. It's about commitment OVER TIME to each other. A commitment that is emotional and mental, even if it's no longer physical. Imagine if relationships were more about truly recognizing that primates will always seek other mates even though you are mentally and emotionally committed to each other rather than about owning, controlling and seeking to stymie your partners natural personal evolution.

Let's look at some examples:

SCENARIO 1

Linda and Carl met through an online dating app. Their first meeting went well, and over time, a relationship developed. They took turns staying in each other's homes for the weekend. The relationship seemed perfect to Linda. They fell deeply in love. They had an excellent sexual/physical connection. Their families were supportive. After a divorce several years early, Linda was very happy and sure she'd found the man she would spend the rest her life with, since she felt Carl was the love of her life. The relationship continued in this routine for a couple of years; taking turns driving to each other's homes, enjoying weekend activities, spending nights having sex and sleeping close together. During the week when work and other obligations kept them apart, they kept in touch through phone calls and text messages. Linda was very happy and planned her weeknights around Carl's calls and weekend around their visits.

One weekend when Linda arrived at Carl's home, he asked if they could have a chat after dinner. Since it was routine for them to sit and talk with a glass of wine after dinner, Linda thought nothing of it. Tonight was different. After sitting down, Carl explained that he loved Linda very much. She was a wonderful partner, and he did not want to end their relationship, but he felt it was time to discuss opening it up. Weekend relationships are difficult and can get lonely, he said. He wanted to go out with other women during the week and he wanted Linda to see other men as well if she chose. Carl reiterated that Linda was his priority and always would be. Carl felt that they should discuss rules for dating others during the week so that both of them would feel comfortable. Would Linda please consider this?

Linda didn't even pause. She felt threatened, hurt and jealous, sure that he probably already had met another person. She accused him of cheating. Carl - who had NOT cheated - of course denied this, but Linda wouldn't listen and/or refused to believe him. She ended the relationship, packed her things and left.

When interviewed, Linda stated "If he loved me as he said, and sex was good, why should he want another person ever?" Linda still refers to Carl as the "love of her life" and has not had as strong a connection or long relationship since Carl.

Many of you out there are probably sympathizing with Linda, thinking the same thing she did. But stop and consider for just moment…you don't have just one friend that you do everything with, do you? Most people have several friends that they do different things with. Some may like to work out, some may enjoy going out to clubs and other may like staying in and watching movies. You would never expect a single friend to do everything with you…besides accounting for different like and dislikes, your friends have other friends too and will do things with them. To meet all your social needs, you have a variety of personality types as friends.

Now let's extrapolate that to a relationship. if you have more than one friend, why would you not want to have more than one partner? No matter how much you love your partner, there may be things that you enjoy doing that your partner just doesn't like and vice versa. When one (or both) of you have to suppress needs or kinks or desires, it builds not only resentment, but makes that desire build to where it may become an obsession. Many times, it leads to one partner (or even both) cheating on the other which destroys trust, and blows apart the entire foundation of a relationship.

What must be remembered is that sex DOES NOT equal love! Sex is an act. Love is an emotion. Sex can be enhanced by genuine feelings between two people, but it isn't necessary. Most people have had one-night stands at some point in their life. Did you love that person? Of course you didn't. You enjoyed a night of sex with them and that's it. As we grow older, for some reason, we lose sight of the fact that sex does not equal love.

We are fed the line by society that we should want to settle down with a single person for the rest of our lives. Going back to the example of friendship - you wouldn't expect to only have one friend for the rest of your life, would you? Of course not. People change…every day. The human experience guarantees that you are constantly bombarded with input, and that input changes you a bit. This doesn't change because we choose a partner and try to dedicate ourselves to only them for the rest of our lives. Needs change, and while that single partner can no longer meet all your needs, that may not change how you feel about them.

Instead of ending the relationship, imagine if you acknowledged that change, and acknowledged the need to have other partners fill needs that a single partner cannot. It doesn't change your partner's commitment to you. In fact, in a lot of cases it can enhance it. What it does do is take the idea of "forbidden fruit" or obsession out of the picture. It allows both you and your partner the chance to explore other needs - physical, mental, social and emotional - while being completely transparent about what is happening.

Think about Linda and Carl. Imagine if Linda, instead of becoming angry and convinced that Carl was cheating, if she had stopped and allowed a fully open and honest conversation about Carl's motivations for wanting to open the relationship. Imagine if she had realized Carl's need to see others was not a threat to his feelings for Linda. Things would have been very different. It's quite likely that Linda and Carl might still be together today, thriving in a situation where both partners were having needs met during the week and enjoying each other's company on weekends.

Choosing to be non-monogamous/poly/open is not the end of a primary relationship. It's usually just the beginning of a new chapter in how both partners perceive each other.

SCENARIO 2

Katherine and Matthew met through a mutual friend. Matthew was very attracted to Katherine and convinced her to go out with him. It took some time, but eventually Katherine began to enjoy Matthew's company and they spent much of their free time together, either alone or with other mutual friends. Katherine was a very "together" person; Matthew was not. In Katherine, he felt he found someone who would take care of him. Katherine believed she saw in Matthew a person who just needed a steadying and grounding influence in order to grow. Their relationship developed very quickly.

Katherine was in her late twenties and Matthew had just turned 30. Katherine's friends kept asking her when she was "going to settle down, get married and start a family". She never had an answer as that never really seemed like what she wanted to do. But at 28, she felt like that's what she SHOULD want, so when Matthew proposed, Katherine, despite inner misgivings, said yes. They were married 10 months later.

From the beginning of the relationship, Katherine knew that Matthew was bi-sexual and would have a need that she could not meet. She always told Matthew that if he ever saw another woman (or man) he was interested in sexually, don't cheat or lie about it. If he was interested in another, they could sit down and discuss opening their marriage. Katherine said she understood that Matthew would have needs or wants that she might not be able to fulfill. She was more than willing to discuss terms and rules for opening their marriage. Matthew would just have to understand that if this discussion occurred, Katherine would have just as much a right to go out with another man if she chose. Matthew didn't like that idea and assured Katherine that he was content with her. Despite his assurance, Katherine reminded him often that he should always feel he could bring up the topic of seeing other men or women.

Matthew and Katherine had very different interests and although they tried to take part in each other's activities, it just wasn't enjoyable for either partner. Katherine always supported Matthew's choice of friends and activities. Her parents had both had very different interests and never tried to stop each other from enjoying them. Katherine felt it was natural to both have their own lives and things they did without one another. Matthew on the other hand, felt that "I belong to my wife, and she belongs to me". He felt that all activities should be done together. This led to many arguments and uncomfortable moments for both of them.

Before they were even married, Katherine understood that there would be times when she would not want to take part in the things he enjoyed doing and that there would be sexual and social needs that she could not meet. She felt it was unrealistic to expect that Matthew would meet hers. This was her reasoning behind making sure that Matthew knew that she would always be willing to have an open and honest discussion about seeing other people.

Despite Katherine giving Matthew the opportunity to be open about being with other people, he cheated on Katherine with both men and women. Understand that cheating is seeing others without your partner/spouse knowing and then lying about it. Katherine had always clarified that if he wanted to have a physical relationship with another person, Matthew just needed to open a dialogue about it so they could create rules/guidelines that they both would follow. He also needed to acknowledge that Katherine had the right to see others too. Matthew did not want to "share his woman", so instead of discussing opening the marriage, he cheated.

I'm sure that anyone reading this can guess that outcome. Katherine and Matthew are divorced. Katherine said this about her divorce: "It wasn't the Matthew cheated. I always knew he would eventually have sexual needs that I couldn't meet. People often get bored with their partners and want to see others, even if they are married. I was always ok with the idea of opening up the marriage. In fact, I would have welcomed it. What ended the marriage wasn't his cheating. What ended it was him lying about it because he wanted to see others, but didn't want me to have the same option."

This raises an important part of non-monogamy. What is good for one partner has to be good for the other. With Katherine and Matthew, Katherine went into it with her eyes open, knowing she was marrying a bisexual man. She wanted to allow him the freedom to see others, knowing that she could not possibly meet all his needs sexually. She often tried to discuss it with Matthew and reassure him that it would be ok, as long as she had the right to see others too.

Matthew had a common mentality in men (and in more than a few women) that being married is like owning one another, and he didn't want to "share his woman" with anyone else. That isn't how non-monogamy works. Both partners have the freedom to see others…within the parameters of whatever rules and agreements the couple agrees upon beforehand. If one partner wants to enjoy the benefits of non-monogamy, but doesn't want their partner to enjoy the same, the result is cheating.

SINGLE AND SOLO-POLYAMOROUS

Society tells us that becoming part of a couple, whether monogamous or primary poly, is what is desirable. Being single is seen as being immature and unsettled, and couples are seen as responsible. Logic tells us this point of view is ridiculous. Is a single person who owns their own house, has a car and career, lives alone and is financially secure less responsible than a couple? Of course not. In fact, perhaps a single person in this is MORE responsible than their couple counterpart as they do not have the luxury of a second income or assistance. But that is a separate debate for another time. For some people, being in a monogamous relationship, or being the "primary" in a poly relationship is all they want. They need to be identified as part of a couple.

What about the people who are perfectly happy being solo? What about those who love the freedom of NOT being in a single, primary partnership, who are completely autonomous and have the self-esteem to be perfectly happy identifying themselves as an individual rather than a couple? Where do they fit into the polyamorous paradigm? Few will be happy being made to feel like second-class citizens with the designation of secondary partner. It's anathema to them.

Never fear…there is a polyamorous situation that can fulfill the needs of a person like this. It is often called "solo polyamory". Yes…that sounds like a contradiction in terms, but it's not…not once you understand the most essential and basic element of the "solo-poly" situation.

Someone who chooses to be solo and polyamorous simply chooses NOT to have a primary partner for a variety of reasons. Perhaps it's the single parent who prefers not to have the time/energy to devote to a "primary" and instead devotes the time and energy that a "primary" partner would demand to their children. Or how about an adult who is the caretaker to an ailing relative? Or maybe a single adult that simply doesn't want the complications and drama that come with having to keep a primary partner happy? When someone chooses to be solo and polyamorous, they are making the conscious decision to devote their time and energy to someone who is NOT a partner per se. They spend their energy developing a platonic/parental relationship with another important person, or they work on getting to know themselves, developing their self-esteem and building self-love rather than doing the same for another person.

For many people, choosing to designate yourself as your prime partner sounds selfish. In modern society, we are taught you should always put others before yourself. This is, of course, ridiculous. You cannot be a good parent, friend or partner if you don't put yourself and your needs before those of others to some extent. If you do not spend the time developing your acceptance and love of yourself, you cannot expect to have a satisfying, healthy and loving relationship with another person. Being solo-poly and choosing yourself as your primary partner means that you recognize this need. In doing so, you spend your energy in making yourself a better and more balanced person, thus making you a better partner for ALL your other partners and relationships, even those that aren't sexual (i.e. parental, caretaker, etc.).

Those that choose to be solo poly tend to value their freedom and autonomy. They are entirely comfortable being on their own to do a variety of activities, from going to the beach to going to a bar. While they maintain multiple committed relationships with their partners, they prefer their own space. They are more than happy living on their own and work hard to maintain that independence. When there are important decisions to be made that affect their partners, they will look for input, but ultimately will make their decision based on their own experience, and will accept the consequences of their actions. Solo polyamorous people don't map out a future with someone, they map out their own future and see all their partners as part of it.

Many will ask what the difference is between being solo-poly and just dating. The differences come in the understanding of these two situations, rather than in the words themselves.

When someone says they are "dating", there is the social understanding that they are searching for a single partner to be "the one". There is the implication that monogamy is the intended outcome; that "couple hood" is where they want to end up. In fact, the whole term dating comes with a boatload of social expectations and baggage that can take what would have been a fun, relaxed interaction to one that is anxiety ridden and awkward. It is expected that when you date, you plan to eventually select one person from many, and stop seeing anyone else. With solo polyamory there is no preconceived end game. Instead, those who follow the solo polyamorous path are content to just let things unfold and enjoy being present at the moment. They will just let the connections happen at a natural pace rather than project a socially driven agenda on the relationship. In solo polyamory, it is the connection that's important–and that connection could follow any of a dozen (or more) paths, and all of them are worth pursuing,

This leads people to say "Well, then that's 'casual dating'." Once again, this may be what the average person who is not solo polyamorous sees, but look beneath the surface and you will find differences. Casual dating has become synonymous with "casual sex". For whatever reason, there is the implication that someone who dates casually will jump into bed with anyone they encounter. This could not be further from the truth for most solo polyamorous people. Remember, in solo polyamory it's all about creating connections to others. Yes, sometimes that may include sex, but not all the time. In solo poly, friendships and intellectual connections are just as valued and sought after, and tend to be as important as the sexual connection between two people. In fact, if you speak with most solo poly people, they will probably tell you their partners are more than just lovers, and that they rarely have sex with just anyone. Rather than being casual about who their partners are, they are quite selective about whom they get into bed with. A solo polyamorous person said the following about this:

"When I meet a new person, there is usually an element of sexual attraction. After all, no one meets up with someone they don't consider physically attractive. Physical attraction is the easy part. What I'm looking for is more than the physical attraction. I want to be able to have a conversation with that person; I want them to mentally challenge me a bit, and I want to know I can laugh with them and have a good time, even if sex isn't involved. Frankly, if I meet someone, and the only element there is sexual attraction, I tend to actually get turned off. That's not to say I haven't had the occasional one-night stand thing– I certainly have. I'm a functional adult. What it says is I won't form relationships that are strictly based on sex. There has to be more, or I get bored and end things before they start."

The socially driven response to the above statement is: "Well, if you are looking to form that kind of relationship with someone, why do you need to have more than one person?"

In solo polyamory, you recognize that people change all the time. They are constantly remaking who they are, or are experiencing some kind of situation that changes them as they learn to adjust and cope. Think about it… who you are today is a very different person from who you were a year ago at the same time. Thought processes, coping mechanisms, priorities, etc. change profoundly in the course of a year.

Polyamory allows for that change in relationships. Because relationships are created and allowed to grow organically, without monogamy/marriage/exclusive dating being the end game, they tend to evolve along with the people. This may mean that a relationship naturally runs its course and partners go their separate ways. More likely to happen is that it deepens. Partners love each other BECAUSE of the changes that occur, rather than despite them. And because love in a solo poly relationship comes with no conditions or strings attached, there is no pressure to constantly be the "perfect partner" (which of course does not exist). Some find that the relationships that start as low key, with strongly connected friendships and little initial chemistry, develop into ones with a strong chemistry, built because it could grow on its own, rather than be forced.

"I met one of my partners, Cyndi, about 6 months ago. Initially we connected very strongly on an intellectual level, but the chemistry wasn't totally there. We became each other's sounding boards and confidantes. We met up regularly just to talk, maybe workout, walk or other outdoor activities. I found that slowly over the course of a couple of months she became the bright spot in my day. I looked forward to hearing from her every morning and she was one of the last people I said good night to.

When we would meet up, I found that chemistry that wasn't there at first seemed to be slowly building as I got to know her better. It took a long time, but eventually we both realized that we had created a strong chemistry and sexual attraction between us simply by allowing the relationship to grow naturally. It's the first time I'd had that happen. In all my other relationships, the chemistry was there right from the start, but in this one it grew and became intense.

In a monogamous standard, or even a casual dating one, I don't think this would have happened. The pressure to find a partner is there in monogamy, and in casual dating/sex, if the chemistry isn't there, you tend to write things off and move on. I think because we are both poly (Cyndi is solo poly, I have a primary partner I live with), we recognized how important the intellectual connection was since it's actually far rarer than a sexual one. Letting things just grow on their own in whatever direction it went is part of our mindsets. The result is an amazing, intense, loving relationship that now includes amazing sex as well."

The final caveat regarding solo polyamory is an often-overlooked part of any polyamorous situation, especially in solo poly ones. Perhaps the most important thing to remember about being solo poly is balance. Balance between responsibilities and partners, balance between existing partners, balance between new and existing partners.

It's very easy to get so caught up in the wonder and loving relationships of being poly that you forget there are other responsibilities you must continue to meet. There is work, home, friends and family. Depending on how much you choose to involve any of your partners in any of these other facets of your life, it's important to make sure that you keep all things balanced so none of the others suffer.

It's especially important to focus on yourself too. If you are choosing to be solo poly, you acknowledge that you do not want to have a single primary partner. You've chosen to focus on someone else as your primary - whether it's your child, your friends or yourself. No matter which one it is, it's vital that you take time for self-love. You need to take the time to step back and focus on yourself. Make sure you step back at least once a week, take a deep breath, and do something for you and ONLY you. Go to the gym, a walk, a swim. Get a pedicure, a haircut or a new set of clothes. Catch a movie, a game, or a band...and do it entirely solo. It doesn't have to be anything big or expensive, it just has to be something that invests in your mental, emotional and physical well-being. Remember...without self-love, you simply cannot open yourself to a strong, open, honest and deep connection to anyone else. Developing that sense of self is perhaps the single most important thing for being poly; a strong love of self that leads to the self-esteem and confidence to love others with no strings attached and in a non-attachment fashion.

Once you have several partners, make sure you balance your time with them. No matter how strong and open a relationship is, it will suffer if you don't make the time to continue to foster it. Again, this fostering should be in all spheres...mental, emotional and physical. Neglect of any for any length of time can lead to resentment or more likely...just drifting apart. Poly relationships are not binding, confining, clingy or needy, yet they do need your time and effort to thrive.

As a poly person, you will be always looking for and meeting new potential partners. It's fun and exciting to meet a new person. New people stimulate the dopamine centers in your brain, and they make you feel different. It's easy to become so swept up in the dopamine effect to the exclusion of other partners. It's normal and natural. However, once you have chosen to be solo poly, you have decided not to set up a hierarchy among your partners...that is, none of your partners is your primary - they are all equal. Be careful to not allow dopamine to create the illusion of a primary partner. When you meet someone new, take the time to reaffirm your bond with other partners too, whatever the nature of the bond is. In the end, it only leads to stronger and better connections that will continue to be open, honest and deeply loving.

Solo polyamory can be a fulfilling and loving way to live. You are free to build loving relationships without the expectation of exclusive "couple hood". You can remain autonomous and independent, while still having relationships that can be deeply loving. It's not for everyone though. As mentioned, you do need to have the right mental attitude. This includes being willing and able to step outside the box, getting off the typical "relationship elevator", and being yourself. Patience is not just a virtue in solo poly, it's a necessity. Strong communication is a must. Realizing that connections are just as, if not more important than sexual chemistry cannot be overstated. Making sure that you don't bring a hidden relationship agenda to the table when you meet someone new is equally important. It's not a lifestyle choice that appeals to everyone, and it's work to maintain, but for those who choose it, it's the only way to live. Katie discussed an example of this...

What is your experience with non-monogamous relationships?

I have gotten to a point in my life where I don't want to answer to anyone, so I date, and develop some connections. I have done the traditional monogamy thing before. It wasn't bad, but it can definitely have restrictions. If I meet a person that I am interested in, I could date them, whether or not I'm already seeing someone else. Who I see is my choice, and my choice only. I want to keep things that way, regardless of how close I get to anyone I see.

What are reasons that you would be for or against open relationships?

I take care of my "today" today, and don't think about tomorrow. If I develop a close connection with someone, I still want to keep my freedom of seeing anyone I want while still maintaining this connection. I live in the moment and see who I want to see, not focusing on where things will go with a person. I just enjoy the here and now and let whatever happens with a person run its course.

If you are open to them, what would you say to someone that is against open relationships if they questioned you about it?

Be open and honest, and if the person truly wants to be with you, he or she will. Take chances, see who you are interested in. Don't worry about details in the beginning. If you develop a connection with someone, the details will work themselves out. If you don't connect with someone, meeting new people is still a learning experience, and can be fun.

BEING FEMALE AND POLY

A CASE STUDY

Society tells us that women "of a certain age" should be desperate to find a partner and get married (or remarried). To be single in your late forties, is to be lonely and alone, unattractive and mousey, unloved and unwanted. Doubly so if you are childless. Most people see a single woman's future as wearing house dresses, hair unkempt and no make-up with a dozen cats twining around your ankles. Being single, female and middle-aged means curling up in a lonely, miserable ball and becoming the stereotypical old maid (although it's not the case with men the same age, but more on societal double standards later on).

The following interview is with a single polyamorous woman and explains her reasons for choosing this relationship path

What do you see as the traditional reasons many women fear being single?

It used to be that older women depended on others for survival. Many women had surrendered their ability to be independent because that's what you did when you got married. The female stayed home and took care of the house and children (if any) while the men went out and supported the family. If a marriage ended, those women had little choice but to find another partner to "take care of them" since often they did not have the skills to re-enter the job market. Or if they did, the disparity in wages made it impossible to support themselves. In this modern era, while women certainly do not have the equality that we hope for, we are much better off than our mothers and grandmothers. Many of us have been to college or trade school and can fully support ourselves…and often children as well. Yet despite these advantages, many women still feel they must have a partner in order to survive and be happy and/or fulfilled.

I am lucky enough to be one of those women who has a college degree and a job I not only enjoy, but also that allows me to have my own home, car and the means to support myself modestly. My parents were ecumenical in their belief of what was "women's work"; I was taught to sew, cook and clean. I was also taught to use a lawn mower, power tools, even how to change a tire or the oil in my car. I do not need, or want, someone to take care of me. It isn't exactly easy to be single in the modern era of ever-increasing taxes and financial demands, but I manage by choice. Yet still despite women's liberation, women's rights, etc., society still pressures women to be married. TV, movies, books, commercials and advertisements, are constantly conditioning women to believe that to be married is to fulfill your purpose. You should WANT to be married and taking care of a family.

Finally, there is a lot of the sentiment "Aren't you afraid of getting old alone/dying alone?" many would ask. Nope. Not even a little. Without getting too philosophical, everyone dies alone. No one can truly be with you when you cross into the void, and I look forward to growing older and the adventure that it brings.

Being a single woman continues to be an abomination in the modern day. Many women (and to be fair many men) want to "belong" to someone. I have never had that desire. I never saw being in a relationship of any kind as giving me any sense of owning my partner. When I hear someone say "that's MY man" or "she's MY girl" it makes me cringe. So…you own your partner like you own a pair of shoes or jeans? They are your partner, so you should have the right to dictate where they go and who they see? Being in a relationship should not mean having to surrender your sense of self or individuality, but that's EXACTLY what women are told should happen. We are told that we should be happy to let go of the things that make you unique and allow "two to become one". Society tells us that losing yourself in your partner is something to be sought, actually desired. Even worse, society tells women that we have more value if we are someone's wife or partner. The message often is that no matter what we do, what we accomplish, single women are less valued or important than those that choose to engage in marriage. The idea of wanting to be someone's wife is the path to gaining respect and respectability and is drilled into us as young girls from all sides. It is so ingrained, we never stop and consider if we really want to be married, or what the alternatives are…or even that there ARE alternatives to the traditional relationship. So, we go along with the idea of getting married - more the feeling of that's what we are SUPPOSED to do, SUPPOSED to want - even if we know it's not really what we want.

Are you against the institution of marriage?

Well, I know I am not good at the whole marriage thing. I tried it, and after 9 years of marriage, I finally admitted I always felt as though I was playing a part rather than living as myself, and ended the marriage. Knowing this about myself is enough to keep me from marrying again. Further, now my views on marriage have changed so radically that I can think of no reason to take part in that outdated institution again.

So why did you get married at all?

I felt it was what I SHOULD want at the point I was in my life. Society was telling me that at my age I should want to settle down with one person for the rest of my life, raise a family, and be happy, selflessly devoting myself to husband and family. So…that's what I did. In the clear, cold light of hindsight, I should have stopped everything. I should have worried less about the money that had been spent, and more about what I had realized about myself. I knew I didn't like my husband to be saying "now you're mine. And I am yours". My response to that from day one was always "No, you don't belong to me and I don't belong to you. We belong to ourselves" That always made him a little upset. It's easy to see now that a traditional relationship was not going to suit me, and if I am completely honest, I can say I wasn't a great wife. But with no other examples of relationship instances in front of me, I got married. Foolishly.

Why share this?

In order to explain that I HAVE tried the traditional relationship that society tells us we should want. Tried it for nearly ten years before realizing I just couldn't continue to play the part of a traditional partner. Being "owned" by my partner made my skin crawl. It still does.

Some people are a little more emotionally and mentally able to cast off the pressures and weight of society and the narrative that is outlined before we even draw breath. We are born with those pressures and that storyline laid out before us, but we can choose whether to follow them. Yes, I was married. Yes, I am divorced. From the moment I chose to end my marriage, I knew I was casting off that storyline and was prepared to go forward with one that suited me. I would never be married again, but deciding not to be married again is a big difference from choosing to be non-monogamous.

So why are you single?

As a female in the "dating scene", this is the single most often asked question I get. Sometimes it's an incredulous remark from someone who can't believe that someone like me is still single. Sometimes it's a serious and literal one. It's one I always answer though…and my answer is "conscious choice".

A better answer is perhaps "why should I not be?" I do not have the pressure of being unable to support myself, and am completely comfortable on my own. I have no desire to be married again and I have no children (nor do I want them). What could a traditional relationship bring to the table for me? Other than avoidance of societal censure, not a damn thing.

That brings us to another point. Many women fear being alone and the stigma it brings. Society automatically assumes that if you are halfway decent looking, "eligible", and are alone that there must be something wrong with you. Nothing could be further from the case, at least for me. I sincerely enjoy my alone time. There are so many books to read, things to learn, movies to watch, miles to jog, weights to lift, games to play…how could I ever mind having the time to enjoy these things? But most people never learn to be alone. They value themselves based on how others see them as someone's parent, or the boss, or whatever. Being happy with being alone is a learned skill, and it's something that requires getting to know yourself. Most people don't want to look too closely at who they are.

What are the most important things to know about being female, single and poly?

Self-esteem is the most important thing you learn when you defy the societal pressure of pairing up to not being alone. You shed the need to impress anyone but yourself. You cease to carry the weight of society's judgement and you frankly stop giving a fuck about what others think of you. You live more for yourself and what makes you happy rather than worrying about what will make some completely random and unknown stranger think you are normal.

It's so important that women take the time to acknowledge they themselves are just as important as anyone else in your life and are worth taking care of and getting to know. After all, you are more than willing to date and get to know a stranger. Why wouldn't you take the same time to get to know yourself? More importantly, how can you get to know another person unless you take the time to know yourself. You end up cheating both yourself and the other person. Or worse, you may taint a potentially positive experience with your own problems and insecurities (i.e. jealousy).

Having self-esteem, learning to be alone and be happy on your own, are all qualities that are important to bring to any interaction with another person. Self-esteem will help to counteract jealousy, and jealousy, as many can attest, is poison to ANY relationship. What is jealousy, but a projection of your own lack of self-esteem? The thought process, conscious or unconscious, is "Why is this person with me when I am not good enough for them? I KNOW there is someone out there better looking/more intelligent/richer/ whatever then I am". This often leads to suspecting any interaction with others that your partner has.

A person with no self-esteem will look for the slightest little break in whatever mental script they have for their relationship, and if a partner "goes off script", it's all the excuse they need to intrude into their partners life - checking text messages, sneaking looks at email, sometimes even following their partner to see where they are going. Accusations of cheating start to fly and resentments form (especially if the partner has been entirely faithful). They start to think "if I will be accused of cheating, I may as well do so, since nothing I say will change their mind". So the cheating begins. Or if it doesn't, the partner eventually tires of the accusations and invasion of privacy and ends it.

Now imagine if that same person has the self-esteem to trust a partner. They don't have a mental script of their relationship because they don't need to - they know their partner is committed to them. There are no accusations, no invasions of privacy. Both partners are confident of the connection and commitment between them, both take joy in what makes their partner happy (this can be called "compersion" and will come back up later). The relationship can progress organically and happily. And if the partners choose to separate, it will be because they realize they have outgrown the partnership and need to move on.

In a perfect world, that's how things would go down. In reality, the lack of self-esteem, the inability to be alone and the stigma of being single perpetuate the first scenario. The result, a series of bitter breakups and often some serious drama, something no one wants to deal with.

(Please note that we are not talking about relationships in which one partner is the subject of abuse. An abusive relationship is NOT one where normal action can be applied. That type of relationship will not be touched upon here except to say that if you or someone you know is in that kind of situation, find support and help in any way you can.)

So, returning the original point of this interview on why I choose to be single, my choice is a conscious one. I am lucky to be in a place in life where I can be independent, so I need not have a partner to survive financially. I spent the time getting to know myself, which led to the self-esteem and self-awareness that I am completely comfortable either being alone or with others.

Some may say "you don't have to be married. Why not look for a long-term relationship rather than marriage?" My answer to that excellent question is that I have decided to not engage in the traditional relationship format, rather a non-monogamous relationship style instead.

THE MENTAL ATTITUDE

You've read what's in this book so far, and you're thinking to yourself "Gee…when spelled out in such a logical fashion, open relationships, non-monogamy and polyamory sound like legitimate alternatives to the traditional relationship escalator." Congratulations! You've opened your mind to the possibility of finding a different and far more satisfying type of happiness. But before you take a step towards this alternative relationship path, stop and reflect a bit. It takes a certain type of mental attitude to walk in this type of relationship pattern.

BEING ON YOUR OWN

As adults, society often values a person through others–simply put, it's often WHO you know rather than what you know. In fact, many people value themselves that way. They identify their self-worth through others. Many people see themselves only as someone's parent or someone's spouse for example. They do not understand who they are on their own. These are the people you see that seem to go from one serious relationship to another without a pause. These are people who never take a moment to learn about themselves.

This isn't a new-age, philosophy book on finding yourself, so we won't be delving into that aspect. Instead, let's just emphasize how important it is to be comfortable on your own. For example. Molly, a single, non-monogamous, polyamorous woman, had this to say about how important being comfortable on your own is to be successful in her lifestyle:

"I didn't get married until I was nearly 30, figuring I should take the time to "find myself" after college, plus my job took me all over the country. I was rarely in an area for more than 6 months at a time–not conducive to forming any kind of committed relationship, even friendship. When I finally took a job that didn't require moving so much, I figured it was time to have an "adult relationship". I met someone, and the relationship got very serious quick. Within 18 months we were married."

Molly continues "He wasn't a bad person, just a bit immature despite being a couple years older than me. He had gone from relationship to relationship, often serious, living together ones, and even had a daughter with one of his former partners. I didn't think about it at the time, but now I realized that he never learned to be independent. He always had someone "taking care of him". First it was his mother, then a series of girlfriends and finally, me. I didn't question this at first."

"In contrast to him, I had been on my own and moving about the country with all my possessions for almost 10 years. Although I formed some wonderful friendships, they rarely lasted beyond the time I lived in a particular area. I learned to enjoy my own company, to follow my own passions/interests and genuinely enjoy being by myself."

"All of the sudden, or so it seemed, I was married to someone. There was then ALWAYS someone in my personal space, always someone who expected to do everything with me. There was now rarely personal time to myself. I slipped into the trap of being identified, or valued as his wife, rather than as myself. I kind of…lost who I was.

When the marriage ended, I happily took the time to be alone and figure out who I was without being someone's wife. I started doing things I hadn't done in years because my ex didn't enjoy them and resented when I did things without him. I'd forgotten how much I enjoyed being on my own, doing my own thing without having someone else wanting to be there. Once again, I could be happy on my own, and I found it was much easier to be with others. I didn't need anyone but me to be happy. I enjoyed, and still enjoy, sharing my interests with others, but I would never stop doing something just because I had to do it alone."

"I think because I am so comfortable being on my own that being non-monogamous/poly is really the ONLY relationship model that could work for me. And when others ask me about it, I tell them it all starts with being comfortable on your own. Because of having multiple committed partners, there will be times when you WILL be on your own…sometimes for days, or weeks, or months…whether it's because of circumstances beyond your control, or because you choose to be. It doesn't make you less of a person to be happy on your own, and it certainly doesn't mean you are lonely–goodness knows I'm not. Realize you are still beautiful, desirable, exciting and fun. Those things don't disappear just because you aren't with a partner. The modern cliché 'you are amazing, and you are enough' applies here."

"I think if you cannot find value in yourself without being someone else's partner, then this lifestyle just won't work."

Modern society often tells us that we should be ashamed of being on our own. How often are those who choose to be on their own asked "Why are you still single?" Apparently to be on your own implies there is something wrong with you–that you must be hiding some dark secret that prevents you from being a desirable partner. Why do we attach a particular stigma to being perfectly happy doing things by yourself?

There are no easy answers to this, other than perhaps seeing someone who can be strong, happy and confident on their own reminds those who are not of their own shortcomings. Regardless, Molly is correct. Unless you can be comfortable and happy on your own…unless you have a strong sense of who you are as a person...unless you can find value in yourself without being only identified as someone's partner, non-monogamy/polyamory may be a very challenging path to follow.

JEALOUSY IS A DISEASE, SELF-ESTEEM IS THE CURE

Ah jealousy, the 'green-eyed monster' (with pardons to all green-eyed people out there!); that bane of monogamous relationships. It's the killer of more relationships than almost any other emotion, probably second only to indifference in it causing divorce (even if only indirectly). It's an emotion that prompts both men and women to do and say things that they would cringe to hear said to them. Many people seem to believe that if your partner is jealous, it means they care, that they love you. There are people who even deliberately seek to make their partners jealous as a way of testing their devotion.

It's disturbing how accepted and even expected jealousy is in relationships. But jealousy is NOT a sign of love or commitment. It's linked to the thought of 'owning' another person ("I don't share MY girl"; "That's MY man").

Let's put this out there right now and clear up some popular misconceptions: JEALOUSY IS NOT LOVE.

Jealousy is a sign of insecurity.

Jealousy is a sign of obsession.

Insecurity

Jealousy, as most people experience, is linked to the internal monologue that questions why a particular partner chose you. It's the monologue that says you aren't good-looking enough, smart enough, don't make enough money, etc. to truly be attractive to your partner. It's being insecure and not valuing yourself as a person. For whatever reason, you feel that you aren't good enough for your partner, which makes everyone a threat to your relationship. You can't seem to believe that your partner sees something in you that attracts them.

People who are insecure often want to do everything with their partner. They are afraid if they aren't there, their partner will realize that there is someone better out there. There is a desire to be a constant presence in their partner's life, to make the other prove they care about them. This type of person may call or text constantly, or create little dramas to focus their partner's attention on them. They become needy and clingy. The neediness, which may initially be endearing, quickly becomes less so, until the partner has had enough. When the relationship ends, it reinforces the internal monologue that you aren't good enough for someone, and the cycle gets worse.

Or, because you are insecure, you look for signs that your partner will leave. You may even "test" your partner's devotion to you. If your partner then goes "off script" from what you expect, or rather want them to do, it reinforces your belief that your partner is planning on leaving, and that they don't care about you and/or you aren't good enough for them. As previously mentioned, that may lead to becoming clingy/needy, and ultimately leads to the end of the relationship.

An example is not 'allowing' your partner to have friends of the opposite sex, because you aren't secure enough to believe that it's friendship. One interviewee, Laura (another single, NM/poly woman) said this:

"I don't understand jealousy as an emotion. It seems such a pointless waste of time. Either a person loves you and wants to be with you, or they don't. If they don't, being jealous of every person of the opposite gender they come in contact with won't help that. I have honestly lost track of how many male friends I have lost because they become involved with an insecure/jealous female.

It's always the same story; my male friend meets a girl, and initially he shares how excited he is, how awesome she is, how he can't wait to tell me all about her. He says that she is totally cool with him having female friends and that we will get together 'soon'. That never happens. Instead, they quickly drift away, and when questioned, they answer with something like 'I have a girlfriend now and she doesn't like when I talk to other women.' I will remind him that we are friends and were before he met this girl. Why should we not be able to hangout just because they are dating? I'm just a friend. The answer is always something like 'I know, but it upsets her." At this point I usually just say goodbye and good luck. I may hear from that male friend down the road when the relationship inevitably ends, at which point I may be sympathetic, but I do not work to renew the friendship.

It's too bad that women and men are so insecure that they cannot let their partners be independent people. They just cannot wrap their heads around the idea that men and women can be friends and nothing more. Those same insecure people are shocked to hear that I maintain several healthy, committed, non-monogamous relationships. They can't understand how I don't worry that my partner(s) will end the relationship because they meet 'someone better'. My rebuttal to their shock and confusion is "Would me being clingy or needy, or trying to stop them from seeing others make them less likely to leave?" Why should my partner(s) not be able to maintain healthy friendships and/or love relationships with others? We are partners because we have a connection to one another. That won't change because they have connections to other people. Being jealous of their friends is the path to the destruction of a relationship"

Insecurity is a huge issue to deal with and can be linked to many things, including depressions and anxiety. Regardless of the cause, the result is the same. Insecurity becomes a self- fulfilling prophecy, and perpetuates feelings of jealousy (and insecurity) further.

Obsession

It's far easier, and just as common, to see how jealousy slips into obsession, and when it does, it's even more destructive, not just to the relationship, but to the people involved. Obsession is still rooted in insecurity. It's also linked to the idea that your partner 'belongs to you" and no one else. Further, obsession can of course lead to very dangerous situations, like stalking.

But let's look at obsession that hasn't reached that point. Being so wrapped up in another person that you are obsessed with their every movement is simply unhealthy. Mike, a monogamous male who has had partners that were close to obsessive, said in an interview:

"I think there is something very comforting about having a girl say, 'that's my man'. I certainly said things like 'that's MY girl' often enough., I never thought about how that thinking could be taken to an extreme.

One girl I dated, Amy, seemed like a great match for me. We got serious pretty quickly, and she seemed to really enjoy telling everyone I was HER man. Initially, I really like hearing that, but over time it seemed to take on an over-the-top possessive attitude. As our relationship went on, she slowly started to become obsessed with knowing who I was talking to, where I was, and who I was with every moment of the day. I had to stop talking to one of my best friends–who is female and hide her contact info under another name in my phone because I just couldn't deal with her constantly questioning me.

Then she activated "phone finder" on my cell so she could track my movements. When I was in the shower or engaged in another task, she would take my phone and look through all my texts, recent calls and voice mails. I found out later she even made a copy of my house key and would come into the house while I was at work and search for evidence of other women being there. It wasn't long before she started accusing me of cheating. There were some really horrible fights. I broke things off at that point.

It took a little longer to truly have her gone from my life. About two weeks after we broke up, I had to go away for business. When I returned, I noticed several items of mine disappeared from my home. Nothing valuable, but things I knew she liked. I couldn't prove it was her, but I suspect it was. I changed the locks right after that trip and there hasn't been a problem since that time.

In retrospect, I can see that the relationship was already "cooling down", and maybe that's what prompted her jealousy and obsession. I don't know for sure. One thing I do understand now is how that endearing comment of 'that's MY man' can go too far".

Mike is lucky that simply changing the locks stopped what could have escalated further into a dangerous situation. The message with both insecurity and obsession as fuel for jealousy is really that the problems are with you and your thought process, not your partner's actions or words. It was Amy's insecurities that meant she couldn't stand the idea of Mike doing things without her. It was her jealousy and possessiveness that became an obsession. Rather than talk about her feelings, she projected her own insecurities onto Mike, and acted out.

SELF-ESTEEM: THE NEMESIS OF JEALOUSY

Insecurity, obsession and jealousy are generally most prevalent in those who lack self-esteem. Self-esteem is the love of self; it's finding your inherent worth as an independent person, rather than because you are part of a couple. Self-esteem is a difficult thing to nurture, no doubt about that. Even confident people may have low self-esteem and have moments where they stumble and believe they are worthless to their partner. That's normal and natural. What separates a person with high self-esteem from someone who is insecure/obsessive/jealous is how they deal with the bad days.

A person who is lacking in self-esteem will challenge or test their partner to force them to prove how much they care. They may start a fight over something their partner sees as trivial. A person who has realized their worth, will realize they are having a bad day and move on.

So how does one nurture self-esteem? There are many new-age and/or psychology books that you can read to explore this. There are even classes one can take. They all have one underlying thread–to love yourself, you must accept who you are and be comfortable in your own skin. Stop caring so much about how others perceive you, stop thinking that you aren't good enough. Learn to love the person you are. You need to accept that there are things about you that are amazing and other things that are dark. There is nothing wrong with not being perfect–and your partner may well love you BECAUSE of your imperfections rather than despite them.

Taking things a step further, having self-esteem means you need to be completely and totally comfortable being ON YOUR OWN. Sound familiar? It should. People who are self-confident will enjoy their alone time. They don't equate their self-worth through their partner (if they have one), and they don't project their own insecurities/obsessions on to their partner. They are people who know themselves well, acknowledge their virtues AND vices, and truly embrace their inner demons.

This is not meant to be a comprehensive examination of the psychology of jealousy/insecurity/obsession. That is well beyond the scope of this book and frankly has little to do with non-monogamy/polyamory. The above is simply meant to present examples of how jealousy is tied to insecurity and obsession and how it pertains to the next section - jealousy and non-monogamy/polyamory.

JEALOUSY IN NON-MONOGAMY /POLY RELATIONSHIPS

Self-confidence and the ability to be alone are essential for those who choose to engage in the NM/poly lifestyle. These lifestyles seem to be a fertile ground for the destructive effects of jealousy. Yet, if you speak to someone who chooses these lifestyles, it will be clear why it is not.

Molly said in her interview: "Jealousy? Yes there can be jealousy in polyamory and non-monogamy. What I believe is different is how people in this lifestyle choose to deal with jealousy.

Initially when one of my partners told me they were going out with another person that night, I would feel a little jealous, but instead of acting out in jealousy, I stopped and thought about WHY I was jealous. I realized I wasn't jealous of the other woman. Rather, I was jealous of the time spent with my partner AND I was jealous of partner for having another person to go out with! How's that for ridiculous?

At first, I wasn't sure how to deal with either of these issues. I did a lot of self-examination to figure out how to deal with this. Most importantly, I talked to my partner(s). It took longer than it should have, but I realized that my partner(s) going out with another person does NOT affect the time I spend with them, or their commitment to me over time. In fact, their going out with others actually *enhanced* our relationship in the long run. I knew that my partner(s) were out having fun with others that were able to provide something that perhaps I could not, but conversely, I provided my partner(s) with something that others couldn't. What a revelation that was...and frankly it was a huge confidence booster. I know that sounds counter-intuitive, but it's true. It made me realize that my connection to my partner(s) was unique and valued–by BOTH of us. It was valued enough by both of us that we could talk about it.

As for being jealous of my partner(s) going out with others, the remedy for that was just as simple and pretty much the same–we shared our experiences with each other. In fact, I found that as connections to my partner(s) deepened, not only did that jealousy disappear, but I started to find that I was turned on by the idea of my partner(s) with others. It got to a point where I genuinely looked forward to hearing about their experiences (and they looked forward to hearing mine) because it enhanced not only our non-sexual connection, but our sexual one as well. I can honestly say I like knowing when any of my partners go out with others now.

I don't think I could have been as open with a monogamous person about how I felt, because there always seems to be an underlying feeling that you can't share why you are jealous with a monogamous person. It's almost like admitting it means you don't trust your partner and that isn't necessarily the case–since I think jealousy is more about how you feel about yourself than the other person's actions/words. I know that the open, honest and transparent communication that is so pivotal to non-monogamy is the cure for jealousy. Sure, I still have the occasional twinge of jealousy, but they pass quickly, or if it doesn't, I feel completely comfortable opening up a dialogue with any of my partners in order to deal with it"

Jealousy often symbolizes some concern beneath the surface. If you feel jealousy towards your partner, take a step back and think about why you felt that. The easy answer some say is "I don't want him talking to that girl". Ask yourself why though. Why don't you want him talking to her? Does she represent a threat? Isn't the connection between you two strong enough that regardless who either of you talk to, you both ultimately choose each other? That is something many people have a hard time understanding regarding open relationships. "I could never do that. My partner is mine" or "I don't want to share my partner" are common sayings when people hear about open relationships. Those two statements are some of many responses that could be analyzed in depth.

66

If your partner is yours, you own his or her body? You control what that body does? Where it goes, what food goes into, and who it encounters? Your partner is yours, so you are in charge of his or her happiness? Your concern should be focused on keeping your own body happy and not someone else's body. If you truly care about someone, you want them to genuinely be happy. If the other person truly cares about you, that person sincerely wants you to be happy too, and will work with you on ensuring both of you are happy. If this trust is in place, there is no ownership of anyone because there is a mutual trust and respect, with no worries, and thus, no jealousy.

FAILURE TO COMMUNICATE

As Molly says, it is not that jealousy does not occur in NM/poly relationships. What differs is in how those in these relationships dealt with jealousy when it happens. Because there is an increased potential to feel jealous when you have multiple partners (and your partners have multiple partners), it may be a good idea to sit and discuss what's going on with your partners, depending on the personalities involved in the situation.

Many people in monogamous relationships shy away from communicating their needs/wants/desires with their partner. Most people don't like confrontation–they seek to avoid it. When jealousy, or any other feelings or problems start to occur in a relationship, people often just ignore the problem, hoping it will go away. Some may make a half-hearted attempt to discuss it with their partner. Or maybe one partner is more than willing to share and discuss while the other is not. Regardless, neither is a productive or healthy attitude to have in ANY relationship, monogamous or not. Being in a relationship does not automatically convey upon each partner ESP. You normally cannot fully know what is going on in your partners head unless they will share it with you.

When engaging in the poly/NM lifestyle, put aside the ego afraid of being embarrassed by your feelings, and open up an honest dialogue with your partner(s). Misunderstandings can crop up (such as jealousy) and in order to maintain your relationships, you must be willing to discuss them. Even before misunderstandings, right at the beginning, both parties should lie out what they are looking for, set up relationship boundaries, etc.

For example, Greg and Cindy are partners–Cindy is single and poly/NM, Greg is poly/NM as well, but has a core/primary he lives with. Right at the beginning, both parties made sure they were on the same page about where things would go. Besides this, they laid out certain courtesies; Cindy can text Greg anytime, but if he is with his core partner, he won't answer right away out of respect for her; Cindy works out each day after work and will not answer a text while busy with her interests, or out with other people. These little things don't seem like they would be all that important to the relationship, and in the overall scheme of things they aren't. What IS important was establishing that they could and would discuss things that could lead to hard feelings or misunderstandings.

Because of this, when new situations arise, they are both more than willing to bring things up and work things out rather than fall into the trap of ignoring things until what is a small, simple thing becomes a much bigger deal.

We know that communication is important in any relationship, but many times more so in the poly/NM lifestyle. There are multiple personalities to deal with and it's important to be as open and honest about your feelings and concerns as possible.

THAT FOUR LETTER WORD: LOVE

There is no doubt that choosing the path of polyamory and/or non-monogamy is thinking outside the normal relationship box. Yet within this relationship model, there is a need to use mental boxes. Strange, yes, but true all the same. It all starts with recognizing a few truths that have become lost in the modern day "romance" society.

The first truth is so simple, so obvious, that many people overlook it. And it causes many of the issues with opening relationships AND jealousy. It is this:

SEX DOES NOT EQUAL LOVE

Read that again. Say it out loud. Think it over. Then say it again. Sex and love are ENTIRELY different things. Modern day romance has convinced many people that they are the same thing, but they are not.

There is no denying that sex is enhanced by having feelings for your partner (beyond that of lust); love may even be one of those feelings, but love is NOT necessary in order to enjoy sex. Or rather, the romantic idealization of love is not necessary for sex.

Modern society tries to tell us the sex shouldn't happen without the concept of romantic love (eros). In polyamory/non-monogamy, you recognize that this is far from the truth. Have you loved every person you've ever had sex with? Most people, if they are honest, would say no (meaning no, they were not romantically in love with every person they've ever had sex with). It's strange how young people realize that you do not need love to have sex, but as we get older and get more ingrained in the concept of finding "the one", we tend to forget that.

Think about any relationship you may have. Do you love your friends? Your children? Your parents? Maybe even a trusted co-worker? Yourself? Of course you do. Romantic love is not the only type of love out there.

The Greeks were perhaps the first to quantify and define different types of love. They believed that there were 7 different types of love. Here are four that are relevant to these discussions:

EROS

Eros is passionate love. This is where the roots of modern romantic love occur, although like with most things, the romantics have taken it to extremes. The Greeks, however, viewed it as a kind of madness–the madness that inspired the kidnapping of Helen by Paris to launch the Trojan War. Modern day scientists would classify it as "the dopamine effect". You could also simply call it lust. It's the type of love that spurs one to do things without thinking of the long-term effects those actions could lead to. Eros is the lust for possession without thought for the consequences, and is what often leads to cheating in a monogamous relationship (it also leads to marriage which, as has been discussed, should NOT be the ONLY endgame for a relationship).

Modern romantic love has added a twist to the concept of eros by insisting that if you experience eros for someone, they must be "the one"–the person who will be your partner for the rest of your life. Eros was never meant to be a long-lasting love. The Greeks recognized the concept of the dopamine effect and knew that it spurred humans to act without thinking, be guided by pheromones and hormones rather than the head. This does not lead to long-lasting love (as the divorce rate in the US will attest). Rather, it leads to a love that has unrealistic ideas of how things will always be in a relationship. Eros needs the constant stimulation of new conquests to survive, so relationships that start in just eros and never develop more are doomed to failure from the start.

PHILIA

This love is perhaps one of the most well-known and pivotal to ANY strong relationship. Philia is the love and goodwill between friends. Even modern romantics seem to recognize the need to be "friends first" in a relationship. It is most often built over a long period of time and involves companionship, dependability and trust (not sex!) between two people. Think about your close friends. It is probably safe to say that you love them (even if you do not tell them). It should go without saying that especially when building polyamorous and non-monogamous relationships, philia should be a part of those connections.

PHILAUTIA

We have already touched on the concept of philautia earlier in this chapter. Philautia is self-love. Self-love taken to the extreme is narcissism, yet philautia is an essential part of the mental attitude needed for polyamory and non-monogamy. You must learn to love yourself before you can realistically enter any relationship. A healthy love of self includes an emotional appraisal of your own self-worth as an *individual*. Once you value yourself as a unique individual, you will find that it builds your self-esteem. You don't worry about rejection or a partner leaving you for someone else because you can invest in others without it impacting how you feel about yourself.

You may feel hurt or disappointed if a relationship ends, or doesn't get off the ground in the first place, but when you have philautia, you know that anyone leaving does not diminish who you are, or your own self-worth. Loving yourself leaves you open to far more growth and new experiences than someone who sees their self-worth only through others. You will find yourself more willing to take a risk, more likely to experience true compersion, be more accepting of others, and more willing to forgive yourself (and therefore others) when there are problems.

Remember that self-esteem is <u>not</u> the same as self-confidence; you can be very self-confident and have low self-esteem. Many politicians and celebrities are excellent examples of low esteem, high confidence.

LUDUS

Ludus is a difficult version of love to define, but it IS relevant and is, without most being aware of it, the cornerstone of polyamorous and non-monogamous relationships. Ludus is uncommitted love. It's a love that focuses on fun and has no strings attached. It has a strong sexual component, yet is a casual and undemanding love. But for all that, ludus is a love that is very long lasting. In order to experience and understand ludus both parties must be mature, self-confident and self-aware/comfortable being on their own. Ludus also contains a strong element of both philia and philautia.

A modern-day adaptation of ludus is that of non-attachment. Despite the name, non-attachment does NOT mean there is a lack of feeling for a partner. It is actually just the opposite. It is love that occurs on more than one level and is not dependent of being loved the same way in return. Modern romantic love tends to be measured and weighed by partners (often because of low self-esteem/jealousy/insecurity). Our society even enforces this notion that love has to be equal on both sides…that it should be quantifiable.

How often have you seen a partner display some extravagant gift they've been given and hear someone say "Wow! They must really love you", as if the giving of expensive gifts is somehow a measure of how much you love someone. Being extravagant is also seen as an acceptable way to create love, and even to keep love alive. But is love something that should be bought and sold, weighed and measured? Of course not. Especially with polyamory and non-monogamous relationships. Instead the love that exists in polyamory/non-monogamous relationships should be non-attachment love.

Non-attachment love, like ludus, is a love that doesn't come with terms. It is unconditional. You don't say "I love you because…", you simply say "I love you". Your love of multiple persons should not have conditions or expectations, and to be happily polyamorous/non-monogamous, it is unrealistic to make love subject to being quantified or conditional. Non-attachment and ludus are really just ways of saying unconditional love. It is love between people that has no expectation of things in return, need not be proven, and need not even be expressed out loud. It is knowing you have a partner that is more than just sexually compatible, but is mentally and emotionally compatible. Love that doesn't add pressure or expectations to a relationship, but simply grows and is understood. It is long-lasting and flexible.

To find your way through the multiple paths and partners that are implied in polyamory and non-monogamy, it is essential that you let go of the concept of eros, of modern romantic love, and open yourself to ludus, philia and most importantly, philautia.

THE SECOND TRUTH

As you now know, polyamory and non-monogamous relationships tend to focus on philia and ludus. When you have more than one relationship, you find that creating a connection that is beyond simply sexual is important. After all, you are open to loving many people, why settle for something that is strictly based on sex? This actually is a great jumping off point for the next important truth that you must embrace to be happy with polyamory/non-monogamy:

INTERCOURSE IS NOT THE SAME AS INTIMACY

You can blame modern society for having equated these two things. Many people think that intimacy is about sex, but it's not. Intimacy is about being able to speak, show and live your truth in front of another person and know that they care you for BECAUSE of your truth, not despite it.

The actual act of intercourse is not intimacy. It can be a part of it, but is certainly not all of it. Intercourse is spurred by a combination of pheromones and hormones (hence the term 'chemistry'). Nearly every single, multi-cellular species on earth engages in sex (originally meant as an exchange of genetic information for the purpose of producing offspring). Higher multi-cellular beings often indulge in the act of sex for pleasure–bonobos, dolphins and humans to name a few. Intercourse is a pleasurable act, but it is not the same as intimacy.

Intimacy is what we keep referring to as "connection". In the polyamorous/non-monogamous relationship, it is a combination of ludus and philia (with a healthy dose of philautia). It goes beyond the simple act of sex. Molly, one of our previously quoted interviewees, said this about intimacy:

"It wasn't until I truly embraced the concept of polyamory and non-monogamy that I fully understood the difference between sex and intimacy. Sex is…sex. It's biology. It's fun. It's a physical release. But it is NOT being intimate with someone.

In the past, after sex I would just get dressed and leave. I wasn't interested in "cuddling" or whatever. There was little talking, touching, or cuddling. I just wanted to go. How is that intimate? Just because we indulged in a natural act of biology? That's not intimacy.

When I realized this, I stopped focusing on just physical/sexual compatibility and started looking for more. I started spending time with partners I could talk to, partners that were my intellectual and mental equals, partners who also wanted more than just good sex. I wanted partners I could talk to about anything or nothing. It's being able to lay naked in bed after sex and have chats about silly things, or shared ideas. It's being able to share experiences and even problems that I have with other partners and know that I will get good, loving advice without jealousy getting in the way. That's what intimacy is…or what it should be. Not sex…intimacy is a connection."

There is no better way to say it. Intimacy is about connection. If you are intimate with someone, sex may never enter the equation, or it may be there sometimes and not others. It shouldn't matter, because as we've already stated, *intimacy is not about sex*. Being happily non-monogamous/polyamorous means taking the time to build connections and become intimate with your partners. It's not about sleeping with as many people as possible. It should be more about finding people you want to spend time with, both sexually and outside of sex. You value connections beyond the physical/sexual.

Wrapping your head around the concept of polyamory is difficult, but there are plenty of people open minded enough to at least consider its validity. However, in order to engage in a successful polyamorous lifestyle, one must be able to open his or her mind and be comfortable with all the topics discussed in this chapter. Another important thing to grasp for successful polyamory is discussed in the next chapter.

COMPERSION

The response "I don't share my partner" raises many questions. So, you are the only one that has a say in who your partner sees? This other person should have the biggest input in who they see, not you. This would ideally be agreed upon between both partners, and if not, then discussed and hopefully resolved. Not sharing your partner with anyone else would not be an issue if that is what he or she wanted as well. What if your partner wanted to see others sometimes? Just because your partner may occasionally see other people, does not mean that you are "sharing" him or her. Whatever you two have together, he or she does not have that with anyone else. Even if your partner went on a date with someone else, that does not weaken the strong connection between you two.

Melissa and Steve followed the standard relationship path when they started dating at first and things were exciting. They clicked, so they kept seeing each other. They became an exclusive couple and were seeing each other now for 3 years. After this period of time, they were having lunch somewhere, and discussed opening up their relationship. They loved each other, trusted each other, and genuinely enjoyed being together, so this was not a tough conversation to discuss.

Melissa and Steve both acknowledged that even though things were great between them, in certain ways, they each missed the excitement of the dating scene at times, yet did not want to end things between them. They discussed what each were comfortable with, so protocols would be in place, and both would be at ease.

Once that was established, they each started seeing other people once a week. They did this with respect for each other, so if the two of them had plans with each other, that came first. Certain nights were usual nights for them to do other things, like Melissa usually went out on Friday nights, while Steve went out on Saturday nights. They saw other people, disclosing their primary situation to others, so they weren't hiding anything. Steve enjoyed meeting people, making new friends and sharing experiences with different people. Melissa was enjoying her experiences as well, but occasionally still had jealousy thoughts creeping into her head. She couldn't figure out why sometimes she was fine with their agreement to see other people, sometimes she was not.

She talked to her good friend Carrie with the hopes that talking about it would help to figure these thoughts out. Carrie listened to Melissa and told her to take a step back and think about what was causing these feelings. They concluded that Melissa was not feeling jealous of anyone else because she already knew her connection with Steve was solid. She did not worry about any girl "stealing" Steve away, because as Steve would say himself, he doesn't "belong to anyone". He is seeing other people occasionally, but returning home every night as he always has.

She concluded that her "jealous" feelings were more about loneliness and boredom when he wasn't home, than bitter jealous thoughts. She wouldn't say anything about him seeing other people at times because that was what they agreed to, and she was seeing other people at times too (even if it was not as often as Steve). Steve didn't have feelings of resentment during these times because he kept himself busy while she was out, so he didn't even think about Melissa out with others.

After talking about this for a little while, Carrie mentioned a concept that hadn't even occurred to Melissa when she and Steve were first discussing opening the relationship–compersion.

What in the world is compersion? Sounds like a fictional word. The accepted definition is: the feeling of joy one has experiencing another's joy; the feeling of joy associated with seeing a loved one love another. It's not officially in an English dictionary, other languages have versions of it. In Sanskrit, the word "Mudita" means "the pleasure that comes in delighting in other people's well-being". In Norwegian, the word "Unne" can be summed up as "being happy on someone else's behalf". Compersion (or Mudita or Unne) is the anti-jealousy. It is really and truly being happy and excited for something that happens to your partner (or partners).

Jealousy as a self-destructive emotion has already been touched on. Jealousy makes a person look at themselves in an even more insecure light than perhaps they already do. Even more distressing is how society has normalized jealousy as acceptable rather than trying to help people focus on alternatives, such as compersion. Society tells us that it is ok to feel jealous because it is such a common reaction, when really, jealousy is tearing yourself down. Society essentially establishes that it is unnatural to take joy in and be excited about someone else's happiness/good fortune with others. It seems like ALL relationships could benefit from trying to focus on some elements of compersion rather than jumping immediately into jealousy.

Compersion is something that is VERY hard to develop but it's beneficial in the poly/NM lifestyle. Molly touched on it earlier when discussing jealousy. She found that as her relationships deepened, instead of being jealous of her partner(s) spending time with others, or being jealous of them having other partners, she started to focus on how happy it made her partner(s) to spend time with others. When she trained her mind to leave jealousy behind and focus instead on compersion, she rarely felt jealousy. Not everyone will get to that point, but simply being happy, TRULY happy, that your partner(s) are happy, is a great place to start. Legitimately being happy when your partner is happy truly shows that you care about that partner.

Regardless of the relationship lifestyle you choose to engage in, it makes more sense to train your mind to feel compersion rather than jealousy (or envy). Jealousy just makes you feel worse and makes you want to lash out at others to make them feel badly. Compersion, on the other hand, makes you feel better–which makes your partner(s) feel better–so now two (or more) people are happy. Which do you think is the better way to live?

Carrie explained to her how compersion was the opposite of jealousy. You are actually happy for your partner to experience intimate times with others. You legitimately care about your partner, so you want he or she happy, but you also experience joy from them experiencing joy with others. This may sound like a strange concept to many, but compersion is true selfless love.

Compersion is not an easy concept to grasp, even for some couples in open relationships. It is easy to be excited for our partner if they received a promotion at work or something like that, but experiencing joy from your partner having intimate fun with someone else? Many people would respond "What are you, nuts?!", but when you have full trust, respect, and care for someone, you want them happy, regardless of whether it is with you or without you. The key to compersion is not viewing other people as threats.

Melissa would be happy for Steve if he had a great night playing poker with his buddies. Instead of this occasional poker night, if Steve had an occasional hot date with a girl, and things remained the same at home between them, she could feel the same happiness for him as if he was playing poker with the guys. Melissa would be happy for one of her friends if that friend had a hot night with a guy, but she shouldn't be happy for Steve if he had a hot night too? What if she was intimate with someone else the night before? Does that change anything? She should want her partner, the man she loves to have the same joy she had, right?

Some people would say "Becoming a couple means only being intimate with each other, no one else." Would it mean that Steve cares about Melissa any less if he was intimate with other people? Some people would say yes, but that is putting feelings in a quantifiable nature. Intimate moments with other people differ from Steve's feelings for Melissa. Even if Steve cared for other people he saw, that does not mean he cares any less for Melissa.

Diving into details within their relationship, what if Melissa and Steve weren't having sex anymore, for any of many reasons? Because the two of them might not be having sex, does that mean both of them cannot have sex at all? Anything from children, work, stress, fatigue, injuries, or illnesses could interfere and lessen a couple's intimacy. They might have developed less desire for each other over the years. Anything is possible.

Regardless of the reasons that had Melissa and Steve talking about seeing other people, they both agreed to it, and prepared themselves for this relationship change. They both still truly trusted, respected, and cared for each other, but Steve and Melissa wanted to branch out and experience different things, besides the bond that they had together. They both wanted each other happy, so they communicated to make sure that both were still in agreement with this relationship change. Melissa and Steve enjoyed their times together still, and as they became more and more comfortable with both seeing other people at times, they legitimately wanted each other happy spending time on that as well.

They hadn't thought about compersion before until Carrie pointed it out to Melissa, so Melissa brought this up to Steve. Steve had an easier time accepting this non-standard way of thinking because he kept himself busy when Melissa went out and didn't think about it too much. After sharing her occasional apprehensions, and then her compersion discussion with Carrie to Steve, Melissa began to embrace the idea. If Steve was going out on a date, she told him to have a good time, and just stay safe and clean.

Steve and Melissa are just one example of the many types of open relationships. In this type of relationship, both Steve and Melissa knew they were each other's primary partner, so regardless of who they saw, they would still stay happily together. Just like any healthy relationship, if either of them had a problem with anything, they would talk about it. This trust was there for each other, so over time, jealousy was not an issue, and compersion actually came into play because each of them saw the overall continued happiness of the partner they cared about.

PITFALLS

Even though polyamory espouses and encourages that multiple committed partnerships are desirable, it's still a relationship model dominated by partners. In most polyamorous relationships, there is a "primary" or "core" partner. Often, it's a husband or wife where the two have agreed to opening their marriage rather than divorcing. Acknowledging the need to be with other people is definitely a positive step in stopping the relationship cycle that often ends in acrimonious divorce. It allows each partner to develop strong and committed relationships separate from the "primary".

Yet what can happen in couples that choose to open their relationships with those who are not careful is that said partners set up an elaborate set of rules and guidelines for being able to see other people…when and where it can happen, how often, etc. Such constraints are simply another way of partners trying to control each another and, being motivated by a lack of self-esteem and jealousy, can still cause one partner to be unhappy in the relationship.

Further, some couples in a poly situation relegate other partners to the position of being secondary or even tertiary concerns, thus negating the professed feeling of love and commitment for these other people. Regardless of how open a primary couple may appear, there needs to be a mutual understanding with everyone involved. Jealousy cannot rear its ugly head, and communication with everyone involved is crucial.

Beware that creating a hierarchy in which partners are "ranked" can set up a feeling of inadequacy and to some extent, hurt among other partners. Other partners (outside of the prime) can be made to feel secondary. It can then become the prime goal of a "secondary/tertiary" partner to become the primary partner. They may become possessive and unable to deal with feelings of jealousy; they may attempt to lie down ultimatums where they insist on becoming the primary partner. This sets everyone involved up to be jealous, stressed and resentful of all other partners.

Being aware of these challenges in polyamory is important because you can't just dive into it thinking that everything will be easy. Any relationship involves some work, and since polyamory involves multiple relationships, this can occasionally mean added effort. As discussed in this book, there can be many benefits to multiple relationships, but just also know of the additional effort often involved in them.

WHERE TO BEGIN

There are various social situations that people are currently in, and the question arises, "If I were to open my relationship, where do I start?" It starts with mutual consent. Just like most substantial subject matters in standard relationships, ethically seeing other people starts with universal consent. Anyone that is intimately involved in your life should be aware and compliant to you seeing other people, and vice versa.

Many people think that they are open to the non-monogamous dating lifestyle, but they are mainly thinking this just from their experience point. Some people say they are poly and then get apprehensive when someone he or she is dating starts seeing other people. This needs to be addressed before you involve yourself in seeing other people. If you choose to live the polyamorous lifestyle, anyone that you see is entitled to do that as well. Besides being upfront in communicating your desire to see other people, you need to remember that if the other person agrees to this, they have every right to do that as well. Yes, there are various types of non-monogamous lifestyles, including some where only one partner sees other people. That is fine, as long as it is agreed upon by all parties involved. If both people want to see other people, then that becomes the protocol. If both agree that only one of them is seeing other people, then that is the arrangement. Adhering to this agreement, whatever the details include, is the key to maintaining stability in the relationship.

The poly lifestyle might sound foreign to some people that only know the monogamous lifestyle they grew up with. The principle is the same though–maintaining whatever agreement you have with the people you see. This is the same *principle* as maintaining loyalty in a monogamous relationship. A standard monogamous couple both have an agreement that they will only be intimately involved with each other. If either partner in the monogamous couple were intimately involved with anyone else, it would be considered a deceitful breach of their monogamous agreement. Polyamorous people have principle agreements as well. Just because they do not have the same agreement as standard monogamous couples does not make their agreements any less meaningful. Whether there is one primary partner, or multiple important people involved, mutual agreements are established, and any violation of these agreements is deceit.

Remember that there is no one kind of relationship that is better than the rest. There is only what is best for YOU. If monogamous love is best for you, then go that route. Monogamous love is no truer than free love, so if you are at all curious about exploring polyamory, satisfy that curiosity.

If you are thinking of venturing into the poly lifestyle, the first topic to address is how it will affect your current situation. The biggest situational change is if you are currently in a monogamous relationship, but want to open this relationship up. This needs to be discussed with the partner first. Some people do not even want to bring the subject up because one, they think their partner would not go for it, or two, the sensitive nature of the topic brings fear of an uncomfortable feeling in the room.

Holding in the thought is uncomfortable though, and even more so the longer that you hold it in. Can you talk to your partner about anything? How strong is the communication level between you two? Try bringing up the topic by asking questions. The question "Honey, how do you feel about each of us seeing other people sometimes?" is a much easier way of bringing up the matter than just by flat out saying "I want to see other people." The two of you should be able to talk about any important subject in a sociable manner.

If both people truly care about each other, then they want the other person happy. If both sides agree on a matter, that is easy, and it becomes just working out the details. If both sides do not agree, then sometimes one side can bend a little to make something work. That is not the case with seeing other people. Having children is an important topic usually discussed in the beginning of a relationship. Involving children in the relationship is an important enough subject that both sides have to agree on it, with no subtle acquiesce. Seeing other people needs to be agreed upon by those involved as well. Just because this was not part of the arrangement when you two initially got together does not mean that it can never happen.

People change, relationships change, things evolve. Sometimes people outgrow each other. Those that do, usually split and move on. What if you haven't quite outgrown each other, but you have become complacent with each other? Maybe parts of the both of you are still fully strong, but parts have outgrown each other. What do you do then? The standard relationship model just keeps things how they are and preaches things like mixing it up, doing different things, or trying other activities to spice things up. This ignores the fact that regardless of what you do, it is still with the same person, so the excitement level is contained.

Comparatively, the same experiences with someone else can seem much more exciting. This is not downplaying the connection between you and your partner. It is just simple human nature that anything new is generally more exciting than if you had already experienced it multiple times. This includes interactions with other people. It is exciting seeing someone new. It is exciting seeing someone that you haven't seen in a while, as opposed to seeing the same person every day. Acknowledge this as a couple and talk about scenarios.

What if each of you went out with someone else once a week? What is the difference between that and the guy going out to watch the game with his buddies? What is the difference between John playing poker with his buddies on Tuesday night or going on a date with Kendra on a Tuesday night? The relationship between John and his primary partner Rachel remain the same at home, and without limiting his excitement of occasionally seeing other people. If Rachel sometimes went on dates on a Friday night, this would not change the relationship between her and John. This was all possible because both Rachel and John talked and consented to this arrangement. If either did this without the other knowing, that would be deceitful and wrong. If they had something important happening on a Friday night, they could do that together. If John needed to work late Tuesday night, he could switch his date night to another night, just like he would switch poker night to another night. Same concept, same arrangement and communication with his partner.

What is the difference? The possibility of intimacy on a date night. This goes back to the trust between John and Rachel. Human beings are naturally attracted to other people, and acting on that attraction is not a bad thing, as long as it is done responsibly and ethically. John and Kendra aren't always intimate when they are together, but if they are, John has enough respect for Kendra and Rachel back home that he ensures that he stays clean. Maintaining clean sexual health involves not only being careful with protection, but communication between anyone he is intimate with. John understandably does not want to risk his own sexual health, but he also must ensure that he does not affect the sexual health of anyone he is intimate with.

Some people have a blood circle that consists only of people they trust to have unprotected sex with. Sex with anyone outside this circle requires protection. Other people have one or two people they establish a sexual trust with, and anyone else, they use protection with. This is another avenue where the guidelines of communication, consent, and trust are important. If both people have those three guidelines in their relationship, any type of relationship style can be successful.

CONCLUSION

"Every decision for something, is a decision against something else."

Many people in monogamous relationships deal with cheating all the time: the fear of cheating, the suspicion of cheating, the discovery of cheating, the aftermath of cheating. Non-monogamous folks recognize that during a lifetime, you can and will be attracted to other people, even if you are in a wonderful, fulfilling relationship. They make room in their relationship for these attractions, rather than allow them to cause anxiety, jealousy, and unreasonable expectations. Living in the reality of knowing that your partners will have desires for others, and acknowledging that these desires do not take away from the connection between you, is a satisfied way to live.

"Sometimes it is hard for us to grasp things that go against all that we are conditioned to believe."

Having an open mind about many things in life can introduce the possibility of various positive aspects that you never even thought about before, often making life more enjoyable. Instead of seeing the world through a black and white lens, it is like seeing it through a wide range of colors. You have a greater ability to love and be loved. Remember to learn, communicate, and experiment with concepts that you are curious about in life, instead of closing possibilities without giving them a chance. There are many possibilities out there just waiting for the open minds to embrace them.

REFERENCES/RESOURCES

Easton, Dossie and Liszt, Catherine A. The Ethical Slut: A Guide to Infinite Sexual Possibilities. Greenery Press, 1998.

Taormino, Tristan. Opening Up: A Guide to Creating and Sustaining Open Relationships. Cleis Press, 2008.

Wendy-O Matik. Redefining Our Relationships: Guidelines for Responsible Open Relationships. Defiant Times Press, 2002.

Gahran, Amy. Stepping Off the Relationship Escalator: Uncommon Love and Life. Off the Escalator Enterprises, 2017.

###

Thank you for reading our book. If you enjoyed it, please take a moment to leave a review at your favorite retailer.

If you have questions for the authors regarding anything in the book, email Chad or Melanie at Polyfolk@yahoo.com

Thanks!

Chad Spencer & Melanie Fernandes

Made in the USA
Coppell, TX
27 August 2021